MOMENT
TO
CONFRONT

A Look at Elijah and the Prophetic Movement

by Lou Engle and Sam Cerny

TheCall.com
LouEngle.com

⊕TheCall

A MOMENT TO CONFRONT:
A Look at Elijah and the Prophetic Movement
By Lou Engle and Sam Cerny

Published by TheCall, Inc.
TheCall
3535 E. Red Bridge Road
Kansas City, MO 64137

TheCall.com

LouEngle.com

TABLE OF CONTENTS

PREFACE
(Lou Engle)

"Ahab!" Elijah thundered, "Hear my words." Ahab raised himself erect on the throne. The room was held in rapt surprise. Elijah's eyes flashed at the king. His mighty voice reechoed from the walls, "Ahab! As the Lord God of Israel lives, before whom I stand, there shall be neither dew nor rain!" Ahab hesitated a moment stunned by the outburst. In that moment Elijah wheeled and strode from the throne room past the startled guards and toward the outer doors. "Take him! Guards! Seize him!" Ahab stood as he shouted the order. And for three years Israel baked under a rainless sky. [1]

In this book, *A Moment to Confront,* my friend Sam Cerny, the director of The Call School at the International House of Prayer in Kansas City, has given us a wonderful, panoramic view of the life of the prophet Elijah. His message has once again touched me at the deepest part of my own heart, for in Elijah I have found a great hero who has encouraged me to believe for a vast spiritual revolution in America and the nations of the earth. Every aspect of his life is a critical element for the prophetic ministry that seeks to turn a nation back to God. I have been impacted so profoundly by Elijah's revolution that I started a ministry in the 1990's called the Elijah Revolution. I am convinced that that ministry was the preparation ground for the birthing of The Call, a "Mount Carmel moment" where four hundred thousand people gathered to fast and pray in Washington, D.C., on September 2, 2000.

It was in 1999 that I found myself seeking the Lord as to whether or not I was to write an Elijah Revolution DNA book that would be the foundational revelation to fuel the movement of The Call. One

---

1 Stephens, William H., *Elijah* (Wheaton, IL: Tyndale House Publishers, Inc., 1976), pp. 71-72

day in Pasadena, California, a prophet named Paul Cain was going to minister at Harvest Rock Church. At that time this man spoke profound words of knowledge, and those who heard were often startled by his clarity and accuracy.

Moreover, that day I asked the Lord to confirm through Paul if I was to write this book which I was naming *Fast Forward*. It was going to be a call to 40 days of fasting leading up to the dawn of the new millennium. The Scripture the Lord gave me to launch this call to fast was Ecclesiastes 11:1, *"Cast your bread upon the waters."* So I asked for a confirmation and prayed, "God shall I cast my bread, my revelation, onto the waters of public scrutiny?"

Amazingly, that night from the stage Paul Cain called out my wife, Therese, by her first name, Joanne. No one outside of our family knew that name. He then said her birth date, and again this was only through knowledge supernaturally granted by the Spirit. He proceeded by the Spirit to call out my middle name, Dean, along with my birth date as well. For us, this was like shock and awe! But then his next words pierced me like a sword, "I see that you are thin and God says, 'Cast your bread on the waters.'" The confirmation could not have been more profound.

In obedience to that word, I along with Catherine Paine wrote the book, *Fast Forward*. We self-published it with eight thousand copies. In many ways, I think it was one of the most powerful little books that I have written. It certainly did not have widespread exposure, but it was foundational for the Nazirite movement that was being born. When Sam asked me to write some chapters along with his material, I felt I was to draw from those original chapters on Elijah from that book. The material is dated, yet the principles and prophetic infusion still live. Elijah's story still needs to be told today. In fact, Elijah's story is as up-to-date in our time as it was in his. The prophet Malachi declared that Elijah will come again before the great and terrible day of the Lord with such power that it can restrain the curse overtaking the nations. The spirit of Elijah is transferable and men and women of generations to come can pick up that mighty, nation-shaking mantle. America needs that mantle today.

The parallels between Elijah's day and our twenty first century are indeed striking. The vile Baalism of Ahab and Jezebel with its financial crime, massive sexual perversions, sacrifice of babies and persecution of the prophetic church is much like the malignant milieu of our governmental, financial and moral crisis in America and throughout the earth. We write this new Fast Forward in hope that a new prophetic generation would arise and lay hold of the spirit and power of Elijah as did John the Baptist, hundreds of years after the prophet Elijah had gone to heaven in the fiery chariot. I believe with all my heart that this mantle is now falling from the heavenly chariot once again.

Several months before the first The Call in D.C., I had a dream in which I was completely overwhelmed with the impossibility of seeing America turn back to God. But in the dream suddenly a scroll rolled down before me and I read Luke 1:17, *"And He shall go on before the Lord in the spirit and the power of Elijah. He shall turn the hearts of the fathers to the children and the rebellious to the wisdom of the righteous."* Immediately I awoke with a jolt, and the Lord spoke into my inner man, "What I am pouring out in America is stronger than the rebellion." For twelve years I have not ceased to ponder the significance of that dream and have continued to pray, "God, send the spirit of Elijah to America, something stronger than the rebellion!"

Now twelve years from the original publishing of *Fast Forward*, I feel we are coming to another stage of Elijah's revolution that I did not include in the first printing, but it is very much a part of Elijah's story. That is the redemptive judgments of the Lord that on one hand break the power of the nations' gods, and on the other, release redemption, salvation and freedom to the lost and oppressed. In the final chapter of this book, we will unfold a shocking revelation that must be judged by the reader. If indeed the revelation is true, then this 2012 and beyond prayer assignment may be just as important as the assignment that launched The Call itself.

CHAPTER 1

HINGE OF HISTORY
(Lou Engle)

And Elijah came to all the people and said, "How long will you falter between two opinions? If the Lord is God, follow Him; but if Baal, then follow him." 1 Kings 18:21

A Door for Massive Change

There are moments in history when a door for massive change opens. Great revolutions for good or for evil occur in the vacuum created by these openings. It is in these times that key men and women, even entire generations, risk everything to become the hinge of history, that pivotal point that determines which way the door will swing.

Elijah was such a man. Born into one of the darkest times of Israel's history, his calling in life was literally to turn an entire nation back to God. At that time, King Ahab and his heathen wife, Jezebel, seemed to be on a personal mission from hell to stamp out what righteousness remained in Israel. They served the vile Canaanite idols, Baal and Ashtoreth, demonic principalities who demanded sexual immorality and perversion in their fertility rituals. In a rampage against righteousness, Jezebel built pagan altars and murdered the Lord's prophets, replacing these spiritual leaders with hundreds of occultic priests, soothsayers, and temple prostitutes. Israel, a nation belonging to the Lord with Godly roots and heritage, had sunk into its deepest moral morass. [2]

---

2 Both chapters 1 and 2 contain multiple excerpts from the book *Fast Forward* by Lou Engle and Catherine Pain (Pasadena, CA: cu@dc, 1999), pp. 22-55

Confronting Ahab and Jezebel

The influence of the demonic power operating through Jezebel was so great that out of millions of Israelites, only seven thousand were considered to be faithful to the Lord. Jezebel had caused them to forsake their covenant with God and was responsible for corrupting an entire nation. In the midst of this spiritual seduction, Elijah strides onto the scene to confront Ahab, Jezebel and their legions of pagan sorcerers. In the midst of unspeakable depravity, Elijah stood as a solitary voice for righteousness. This one holy man was God's answer to the cohorts of hell hosted by Jezebel!

> "…We must understand these two adversaries as they are seen in the Scriptures. Each is the spiritual counterpart of the other. Is Elijah bold? Jezebel is brazen. Is Elijah ruthless toward evil? Jezebel is vicious toward righteousness. Does Elijah speak of the ways and words of God? Jezebel is full of systems of witchcraft and words of deceit. The war between Elijah and Jezebel continues today. The chief warriors on either side are the prophets of both foes; to the victor goes the soul of our nation."[3]

When Jezebel's influence is felt in the land, prophets have to hide in caves ostracized, but even then they are not silenced.

> A woman was forced off a Seattle bus for having a private conversation about God. Michelle Shocks was traveling on a city bus… when a man embarked and, thankful to be out of the rain, said, "Praise the Lord." Shocks and the man reportedly began to discuss their churches, their Christian faith, and other religions… The driver called Shocks to the front of the bus and told her she could not talk about religion because other passengers might be offended… Shocks moved closer to the man so she could speak more

---

3 Frangipane, Francis, *The Jezebel Spirit* (Cedar Rapids, IA: Arrow Publications, 1991), p. 18

quietly, but was again called to the front of the bus and
ordered to get off. Shocks, who was five months pregnant,
reportedly had to walk along a highway during rush hour in
the rain for about a mile. [4]

The church must come out of the closet and refuse intimidation.
The political cry of this nation is toleration. Today, toleration means
more than, "We accept you as you are, even though we may disagree."
The new definition for tolerance is, "Not only do we accept you,
but your views are true if you believe them." From this perspective,
any belief system is valid and good, no matter where it originated.
But Christians base their lives on truth as revealed in the Bible and
must stand unflinchingly for that truth, even unto death. This is
where martyrs are born. When Jezebel rules, every perversion is
permissible, even encouraged, but just don't force your morality on
anyone. Stay in your church but don't bring your religion into the
public square. Have you felt, as I have, that spirit of fear when you
sense the nudge to witness to someone? Hello, Jezebel.

Jezebel's personal slaves were eunuchs, men who had been
castrated. The word "eunuch" means neutered. These men were
neutralized, unable to stand against Jezebel's power. They had no
conviction. Yet the day came when they freed themselves of her
tyranny. When Jehu, the new king, came to her tower, he gave the
eunuchs a choice: *"Who is on my side? … Throw her down!" (2 Kings
9:32-33)* Those whom she had once enslaved brought about her
downfall.

Those living under Jezebel's domination will always have to
choose where their loyalty lies. When the nation assembled at Mt.
Carmel, Elijah confronted them with a piercing question, *"How long
will you waver between two opinions? If the Lord is God, follow him,*

---

4 *Religion Today*, April 16, 1999, www.religiontoday.com

but if Baal is God, follow him." (1 Kings 18:21) Instead of rallying to Elijah's call, their response is apathy, "And the people said nothing." This was the silent majority who had been defiled by sexual immorality, seduced by false gods and silenced by intimidation. That same silent crowd lives in America. But fire is about to fall again and when it does, a great cry will erupt, "The Lord, He is God!" (18:39)

When we speak of "the spirit of Elijah" or "the spirit of Jezebel", we are not referring to the human spirits of these specific individuals. Rather, we mean the spiritual power that they submitted to, be it the person of the Holy Spirit or the demon gods of the Canaanites. The spirit of Jezebel can just as easily influence a man as the spirit of Elijah can empower a woman. This is not an issue of gender, but one of personal purity and spiritual allegiance.

The prophet Malachi tells us, "See, I will send you the prophet Elijah before the great and dreadful day of the Lord." (Mal. 4:5) The spirit of Elijah must come because Scripture says so! Francis Frangipane says, "Let it be known that if Elijah is coming before Jesus returns, so also is Jezebel."

The Elijah Revolution

In Ahab's time, Hiel of Bethel rebuilt Jericho. He laid its foundations at the cost of his firstborn son, Abiram, and he set up its gates at the cost of his youngest son, Segub, in accordance with the word of the Lord spoken by Joshua son of Nun. 1 Kings 16:34

Jericho was a city cursed by God for its idolatry and had been completely destroyed. Yet in the days of Ahab and Jezebel, the ancient strongholds of idolatry were restored – at the cost of children. Today it is no different. The worship of fertility deities continues under different faces today, in the curse of pornography, sexual abuse and promiscuity that is devastating our children. Once again, the ancient gods are reasserting themselves. Across the earth there is a resurgence of paganism and idolatry, of witchcraft and spiritism. No wonder, then, that the spirit of Elijah is promised to us at the dark close of the age, before the great and terrible day of the Lord!

Elijah's mandate was to bring about a heart revolution: turning the hearts of an entire nation back to God and turning the hearts of both fathers and children to each other. Despite violent opposition from a culture of paganism, he was determined to turn his nation back to God. And the Bible promises us that God will once again send this transforming Spirit.

We will recognize this revolution by five main characteristics:

1. Massive gatherings for national and personal repentance – Elijah summoned the people to Mt. Carmel to demonstrate their allegiance to God's covenant with them. Throughout the Scriptures, in times of great crisis, God called for huge gatherings of fasting, repentance and covenant renewal. Every generation must renew the covenant for themselves. Now is the hour for this generation to decide to follow the Lord.

2. Urgent prayer for a fatherless generation – Elijah revealed the Father's heart for the youth as he stretched himself out in prayer to raise a widow's son from the dead. Dying and abandoned by their fathers, this young generation needs relentless intercession to raise them from the dead.

3. Prayer for revival – Elijah contended for the soul of the nation through prayer. Both fire and rain fell in response to his cry. We need the fire of holiness and the rain of revival in a nation that had been seduced by Jezebel.

4. Extended fasting – Elijah's 40 day fast broke the spell of Jezebel's intimidation. It was the catalyst that prepared Elijah to hear the "gentle whisper" of God and receive his most important commission: to pass the revival mantle to the next generation.

5. A mentoring movement – Elijah anointed Elisha and spent the last years of his life mentoring his double-portion son, establishing the fathering movement Scripture calls "the sons of the prophets," which impacted the entire society. Now is the hour for a prophetic generation of Elishas, who are given to extreme devotion to God, to be raised up.

6. The redemptive judgments of God – For three and a half years God sent a drought no rain or dew came upon the land. The nations' economy was destroyed. God used this judgment to break the back of the shedding of innocent blood, witchcraft and the false religious system of Baal worship.

7. A reformation movement – A movement that overthrows the old regime and establishes a new government that honors God's laws and enacts justice. Jehu was anointed by God to sweep away Ahab and Jezebel's governmental tyranny. Here in America we are not talking about a theocracy, nor are we talking about violent revolution. God's desire is that righteous men and women lead nations so that its people may live in peace and well-being. In every sphere of society God wants to raise up these leaders.

Given that we stand on the threshold of this historic revolution, what must we do? How do we wage this spiritual war? What did Elijah do? Let us walk in his footsteps down the road of radical prayer, fasting and purity.

CHAPTER 2

WAGING WAR
(Lou Engle)

Then he cried out to the Lord... 1 Kings 17:20

Raising a Dead Generation

Then the Lord heard the voice of Elijah; and the soul of the child came back to him, and he revived. 1 Kings 17:22

As we look at all the unholy chaos in the world in these days, we sense that new levels of faith and prayer will be needed to reach this next generation – something close to raising the dead. Elijah's revolution is a prayer revolution. Before he prayed for fire to fall from heaven, he prayed to raise a fatherless child from the dead.

There is an entire generation of fatherless children out there who need to be raised from the dead, so to speak, delivered from spirits of suicide, depression, despair and violence. They are old before their time and many do not believe they will live long enough to see adulthood.

When studying the Bible, we often find that the very first time a word or concept is used, it is usually in a way that defines its meaning or sets a pattern for understanding it. Thus, we can learn about raising the dead by studying, in particular, the first instance of this. In the Bible, the first person raised from the dead was not a king or a priest or a general. It was a poverty-stricken widow's son who had just been on the verge of starvation.

Twice the prophet carried the dying boy in his arms – once up the stairs and then back down again (1 Kings 17:19-23) To raise this generation will take the labor of prayer. We are going to have to carry them to a place of healing. They come with more "baggage" than any generation previously born. To fulfill the law of Christ we will have to bear their burdens. Elijah took the boy to the upper room, laid him on the bed and stretched himself over the boy three times, crying out to God for his life. The "Upper Room" of prayer is still God's answer for dead individuals. He will still visit these persistent prayer meetings with mighty wind and tongues of fire. Let The Upper Room Network (T.U.R.N.) arise all over this nation, where saints would stretch themselves out in prayer for a dead generation in order to TURN them back to God. It took perseverance to raise that dead boy back to life - and it took personal contact.

One family's "upper room" prayer changed the life of my friend and former pastor, Dr. Che Ahn. While still a teenager, Che threw himself into the rebellion of the sixties. As a Korean hippie and drug pusher, a turn was needed. A young girl in his neighborhood saw Che and told her father about him. This family felt a burden for his salvation and every mealtime, they prayed for him. Soon afterwards, Che encountered Jesus in a remarkable way. Since then, he has led thousands and thousands to Christ.

Fast Forward

So he arose, and ate and drank; and he went in the strength of that food forty days and forty nights as far as Horeb, the mountain of God. 1 Kings 19:8

To his life of prayer, Elijah also added a fasted lifestyle. For years, I have been gripped with a vision of the body of Christ fasting corporately. I had stumbled on an old book by Franklin Hall, written in 1946, that confirmed to me that a massive move of united fasting would release unprecedented power and revival. His book, *Atomic Power Through Prayer and Fasting*, launched a fasting and prayer revival across America and the world, as thousands went on extended fasts. Up until then, long fasts had been unheard of.

12

In 1947 God responded with the healing revivals and in 1948 with global outpourings that birthed many of the great ministries of the twentieth century, including Billy Graham, Bill Bright and Tommy Hicks in Argentina. Israel also became a nation at that time.

I believe that there is greater spiritual significance to the extended 40 day fast than we have yet realized. Some of the early church fathers taught that Christians should follow Jesus' example of fasting 40 days. The men who appeared on the Mount of Transfiguration, Jesus, Moses and Elijah had all completed 40 day fasts. If the most bitter battles we fight are against temptation and the evil one, then extended fasting is the atomic weapon in our arsenal! Jesus prepared himself to overcome Satan by going on a 40 day fast. If we can say with Jesus, *"the prince of this world is coming but he has nothing in me,"* then we stand in a place of spiritual authority.

Extended fasting can produce a breakthrough where other methods fail. Elijah's experience with the forty day fast is a clear example of this. Elijah had just witnessed one of the most dramatic demonstrations of God's power, yet despite this incredible victory on Mt. Carmel, Jezebel was still alive and dominating the land. Imagine being discouraged after seeing supernatural fire blaze down on your sacrifice! Talk about an "altar" call! Furious about the death of her prophets and under the possession of the spirit of Ashtoreth, Jezebel vowed to kill Elijah, who ran for his life.

At this point, many people believe that basically Elijah failed and lost his calling, and the Lord had to give his mantle to someone else. No! It is my conviction that God used this failure to position Elisha and Jehu, leaders of the next generation who would remove Jezebel. The angel found Elijah on the verge of collapse and after feeding him, the Lord initiated a forty day fast as Elijah journeyed to Mt. Horeb. Elijah returned to the same place where Moses, generations before, had fulfilled his own forty day fast. I believe that this forty day fast was an act of spiritual warfare against Jezebel's sorceries and that still today, the forty day fast will cleanse us from her influences.

While contemplating the significance of a nationwide 40 day fast, I was surprised to read that in 1971 Francis Frangipane was led through a 40 day cleansing of the works of Jezebel in his life. His booklet *The Jezebel Spirit* is a must read for the church in understanding our warfare against this demonic spirit.

Moreover, in the book, *The Prophetic Whisper*, Richard Gazowsky shares the significance of a 40-day strategy that the Lord gave him. One day Gazowsky and his wife were praying at San Francisco Bay. Suddenly a massive swarm of flies attacked his wife and she ran into the car for refuge. She had been praying for a woman tempted with committing adultery. Gazowsky was suddenly apprehended by the word of the Lord, "I am going to show you a secret vulnerability in Satan's kingdom. His weakness is in the flies."

Gazowsky continues this personal account and writes, "Later that day, we went to the Carmel Public Library, and looked up the word 'fly'…I discovered that the meaning of Beelzebub, one of the names of Satan is, 'Lord of the flies.'….Scientists have discovered that flies have a reproductive period that lasts from four hours to over forty days depending upon the species. When pest controllers go to eradicate flies in a certain area, they spray pesticides every day for a forty-day period. If they destroy the reproductive cycles of presently existing flies, they can kill off a whole generation of future flies. I then saw what God was trying to show me… if a Christian will pray consistently for a forty day period he will be able to conquer most satanic strongholds in his life." [5]

The forty day fast is to turn us back to the original place of covenant. Not only did the forty day fast break the power of Jezebel's

5 Gazowsky, Richard, *The Prophetic Whisper* (San Francisco, CA: Voice of Pentecost, Inc., 1996), pp. 29-30

intimidation and influence, more importantly, it prepared Elijah to receive the most important commission of his life: to anoint Elisha. Whereas before, the Lord was in the fire at Carmel, now on the mountain, *the Lord was not in the fire!* (1 Kings 19:12) He was in the still, small, prophetic whisper. We have to understand that our battles – and our victories or defeats are multi-generational. Without Elisha, the double-portion son, Elijah's commission to turn the nation back to God and rid the land of Baal worship remained unfinished.

Sons and daughters finish the work of their fathers. Here is where we've missed it before. The quick burn of revival is not enough. One generation receives the outpouring of revival but loses it in the next generation. We must have the quick burn of revival and the slow burn of fathering the next generation. Between the fire and the fathering stand the forty day fast. I do not believe the great reversal we long for will come in America without the forty day fast. It is interesting that Moses fasted forty days and had a spiritual son named Joshua, which means "the Lord is salvation." Elijah fasted forty days and fathered a double portion son, Elisha, "the Lord saves." And John the Baptist fasted throughout his life and prepared the way for the greatest double portion Son, Jesus, "the Lord is salvation." Both the spiritual fathers and the double portion Son fasted for forty days.

What would happen in America, if for forty days, we sealed the electronic cultural sewer that flows nightly into our living rooms and spent our strength seeking the Lord? What if tens of thousands of spiritual fathers and mothers across our nation fasted for forty days, repenting and cleansing themselves from inward toleration of sexual immorality, addiction to food and entertainment, closing the windows of hell in their homes? Let these parents pray daily, for forty days, for their spiritual and physical children, to break off rebellion and for deliverance from addictions, freedom from demons, healing for disabilities and hope for the depressed and the suicidal.

The Bible is clear that sexual abstinence is appropriate for prayer (1 Cor. 7:5). What if parents across America would abstain for forty days in identificational intercession for their own children, who have no alternative but sexual purity? How can we call them to abstinence, if we ourselves cannot? The days of illusions are over. There will be no fire in America where there is no sacrifice in the Elijah fast.

Let a young generation of Elishas fast for forty days, to be cleansed from lust, TV addiction, pornography, spiritual mediocrity, and rebellion towards their parents, believing for a double portion of the Holy Spirit to rest on their lives and ministries.

> Fasting begets prophets and strengthens strong men.
> Fasting makes lawgivers wise; it is the soul's safeguard, the
> body's trusted comrade, the armor of the champion, the
> training of the athlete. Basil, Bishop of Caesarea (AD 330-
> 379)

As A Living Sacrifice

In 1999, the Spirit began to lead me into my own 40 day fasting journey that would shape and shake my world, move the powers in California, and give me faith that there are no safe places for the devil. A young woman from Peru came to me and shared a dream that she had received. In the dream, she saw a Roman war goddess in a body of water heaping up huge waves. People were swimming in the rough waters but could not make it to their destinies because of these great waves. But then, in the dream, an angel appeared to her and spoke, "The only thing that can break the power of this spirit is 40 days of fasting like Jesus."

She turned to me and asked, "Does this dream mean anything

to you?" I responded with a deep sense of wonder at the dream. "I believe it is significant. There is a Roman war goddess on the state seal of California, and it is seated on San Francisco Bay."

Now I am not looking for demons everywhere, but there are times that God reveals to us the spiritual powers that must be challenged if the people are to be liberated from the strongman's hold. I found out that that Roman war goddess was Minerva, and one of her attributes was that she made war on men. Welcome to San Francisco. She was also the goddess of wisdom, arts and education. Welcome to California.

As I considered this dream, I was shaken by its implications. If it is a true dream, then there is a demonic spirit dominating California and keeping its people from their destinies. Furthermore, if it is a true dream, then the power of that spirit can be broken. For three years I waited and pondered the dream, and then in November of 2002, we held The Call in Seoul, Korea. Afterwards, I flew immediately from Seoul to San Francisco where we were going to hold The Call in early 2003.

On the flight, suddenly the dream came crashing in to my spiritual radar. The most intense desire to fulfill that dream and break that spirit came upon me. The Holy Spirit was putting His faith in my heart that the "Jezebel spirit" over California could be broken if I entered into Jesus' fast. But then I thought, "I've never done a 40 day fast on water, like Jesus," and I began to worry and reason in my mind, "I could die if I fast 40 days on water!" I was deeply troubled and wrestled within myself. "I want to do this fast, but I cannot die. I've got seven kids."

Very strongly, the Lord spoke to my heart, "Do you love California enough to die for it?" The question pierced me. I was being drawn into an intercessory stand that was much more than just a desire or a prayer. By definition, true intercession is standing in between even unto death. Isaiah 53 speaks of Jesus making intercession at the cross. Prayer is a petitioning of Heaven, and God may answer that prayer. In intercession, though, we are suspending our very being to lay hold of the answer. We present our bodies as a living sacrifice.

Inwardly I answered the Lord's question, "I hope I love California enough to die for it. But I cannot die. I have seven children. You've got to confirm to me that this is You." Three days later, I flew back to California. And on the morning of my 50th birthday, I met with the young man who was married to the Peruvian lady that had the first dream. Knowing nothing of my journey, the first words out of his mouth were "My wife just had another dream. In the dream a woman came to her and said 'Lou is fasting the fast you dreamed about three years ago. He thinks he's going to die, but he will not die.'"

Instantly I was moved into a realization that this was no longer just a good idea. This 40 day assignment was a mission from Heaven, and faith was being injected into my soul strengthening me for its fulfillment. I felt as if the word to me was like the 'angel food' given to Elijah. *"Arise and eat, because the journey is too great for you.' So he arose, and ate and drank; and he went in the strength of that food forty days and forty nights." (1 Kings 19:7-8)*

A Time to Confront

Of course, I launched into that fast. The counterpart to Minerva in the Biblical understanding would be the spirit of Ashtoreth, or the spirit of Jezebel. One of the great tools of Jezebel to reduce a mighty man of God into a whimpering eunuch is to seduce that man into sexual immorality. That same spirit that was alive during Elijah's time was manifested again in the church of Thyatira:

And to the angel of the church in Thyatira write, "These things says the Son of God, who has eyes like a flame of fire, and His feet like fine brass: I know your works, love, service, faith, and your patience; and as for your works, the last are more than the first. Nevertheless I have a few things against you, because you allow that woman Jezebel, who calls herself a prophetess, to teach and seduce My servants to commit sexual immorality and eat things sacrificed to idols. And I gave her time to repent of her sexual immorality, and she did not repent. Indeed I will cast her into a sickbed, and those who commit adultery with her into great tribulation, unless they repent of their deeds. I will kill her children with death, and all the churches shall know that I am He who searches the minds and hearts. And I will give to each one of you according to your works. Now to you I say, and to the rest in Thyatira, as many as do not have this doctrine, who have not known the depths of Satan, as they say, I will put on you no other burden. But hold fast what you have till I come. And he who overcomes, and keeps My works until the end, to him I will give power over the nations – 'He shall rule them with a rod of iron; they shall be dashed to pieces like the potter's vessels' - as I also have received from My Father."
Rev. 2:18-27

This same spirit that worked through Jezebel was now working through a false prophetess who was teaching a false doctrine of sexual tolerance in the church. But Jesus steps into the scene and reveals himself to John the Revelator as the one who has blazing eyes of fire and feet of burnished bronze. Here Jesus comes to His bride, not with tenderness and meekness but in the fires of holy jealously and judgment to cleanse the toleration of Jezebel among his people. Here we read the red letter edition of Jesus' words, *"I have given her time to repent but she would not; therefore, I will cast her into a sickbed..."* *(Rev. 2:22)*

But then the eternal son of God roars, *"But to he who overcomes, I will give him authority over the nations."* I realized in examining this Scripture, that I would have no authority to bind that spirit of Jezebel over California if that spirit had any authority over me. I had to be in Christ Jesus and in His authority, but not just positionally over the powers but also experientially. When Jesus went to the cross to bind Satan, He illustrated the same principle, *"The prince of this world cometh but he has nothing in Me." (John 14:30)*

So for 40 days, I went on this fast, almost completely on water. Every day, I would ask Jesus to cleanse me of inward toleration of Jezebel. I was not talking about pornography, but the One with blazing eyes of fire was searching my heart and my mind, my thoughts and my meditations. I would cry to the Lord, "Cleanse me! Cleanse my thoughts! Cleanse my glances!" And then every day I would take my stand in the spirit of Ephesians 6:10-12:

> Finally, my brethren, be strong in the Lord and in the power of His might. Put on the whole armor of God, that you may be able to stand against the wiles of the devil. For we do not wrestle against flesh and blood, but against principalities, against powers, against the rulers of the darkness of this age, against spiritual hosts of wickedness in the heavenly places.

I would actually see myself clothed in the righteousness of Jesus, standing before that principality, declaring "In the name of Jesus I lift up the victory of the Cross over Jezebel in California."

On the 31st day of that fast and that stand, I found myself preaching in San Diego, the very place where that book *Atomic Power of Prayer and Fasting* was written. I taught the saints of San Diego that their redemptive gift was to win the battle of the heavens through fasting and prayer and to release atomic power to the earth. At 1 o'clock that morning in a San Diego hotel, I had one of the most profound dream encounters I have ever experienced. In the dream I was flying over California, and the Spirit of God was roaring through me the victory of the cross over Jezebel in that state. It was unbelievable freedom and unrestrained power. I woke up under that same sense of the Lord's authority, roaring the victory of the cross. I knew that something had broken, that Satan had been challenged and in some measure his power had been broken. I was actually thinking that this was a Daniel 10 type of breakthrough where the demonic power had to give way and the angel of the Lord had broken through.

The next morning, I flew from San Diego to St. Louis. My friend picked me up at the airport and said "Lou, I had a dream of you at 3 o'clock in the morning." The two hour time difference from California meant that he was dreaming the same time that I was dreaming. He continued, "I heard a voice saying, 'Because Lou has been faithful on this fast, I have given him authority over Jezebel into the nations. And wherever The Call goes I will establish my house of prayer.'" The word given in the dream came from the very Scripture that I had based my prayer stand on, for if I could overcome Jezebel through Christ's strength, I'd gain spiritual authority in California. God was giving me powerful confirmation of the breakthrough. Soon I would see the results and the trajectory of that victory.

The Supremacy of Christ

After the fast in early 2003, I was in Sacramento mobilizing for the soon coming The Call San Francisco. A young man walked up to me and said, "Lou, I heard you speak about dreams, so I prayed that God would give me dreams. He gave me a dream where I saw a stadium filled with people and there was a platform where kings would decree the word of the Lord. Lou, you were there on that platform making decrees, and in the dream the governor of California, Gray Davis, was seated in the stands. Even though he didn't want to, he had to submit to every word you were speaking from the platform with the authority of a king."

Our church at that time had been praying for the governor of California because he was passing bills sanctioning abortion and homosexual marriage. He was an Ahab in California, and the spirit of Jezebel was having her way with him. Right after The Call San Francisco, a process outside of the state's normal election cycle began, and it was called "the recall." California then voted to impeach that man, Gray Davis, out of office.

Could it be that two stadium gatherings and 40 days of fasting bound the spirit of Jezebel and removed a governor from his position? We believe that prayer was a part of that great shaking. Furthermore, the trajectory of that 40 day fast pointed me like an arrow right into San Francisco, the very place that that Roman war goddess was exposed, the spirit that made war against men.

In 2004, I was invited to go to San Francisco to preach at an African-American church. I spoke about the Elijah-Jezebel showdown and about the homosexual agenda that was being powerfully promoted from San Francisco. As I was speaking, a tall white man walked in and sat down in the front row. I didn't know who he was, but everyone was looking at him.

At the end of my message, the pastor said, "The mayor of San Francisco is here today. He has just been elected and he wants to say something." The tall white man was the newly elected mayor, Gavin Newsom. After he spoke, they asked me to pray for him, so I laid my hands upon Gavin Newsom, and prayed something to the effect, "Lord I thank you that all government is derived from your government; therefore, let this man know he will be held accountable for everything he does in this city under the government of God."

Thirteen days later Gavin Newsom began to marry homosexual couples illegally in California. In the spirit of Psalm 2, *"Be warned you kings, tremble you judges of the earth,"* God sent a man to him in love to warn him that he will held accountable. I didn't realize that in my 40-day fast God was thrusting me into a spiritual and ideological battle for the soul of the nation. I was being prepared to raise up prayer movements to contend with abortion and the homosexual agenda.

God has given me a life mandate: to raise up a generation who will give themselves to extended fasting and prayer for breakthroughs against the spiritual forces of wickedness in the heavenly places. The last days generation, as even described in Revelation 12, will so command air supremacy that Satan will lose his position in heaven and be cast down to the earth because he will not be strong enough to resist any longer. Once again the voice of Jesus will be heard in every place where darkness and injustice boasts of its dominion, "I saw Satan fall like lightning."

So from this overview of Elijah's confrontation with Jezebel and revolution in Israel as laid out in these first two chapters, let us now dive deeper into his story and consider the details of his life. Why did he walk in such power? How did he maintain such a strong character? What were the keys to his success? What were the results of his ministry?

CHAPTER 3

THE SPIRIT AND POWER OF ELIJAH
(Sam Cerny)

He will also go before Him in the spirit and power of Elijah, "to turn the hearts of the fathers to the children," and the disobedient to the wisdom of the just, to make ready a people prepared for the Lord. Luke 1:17

A People Prepared

John the Baptist foresaw the coming of the Son, *"One mightier than I is coming,"* and the outpouring of the Spirit, *"He will baptize you with the Holy Spirit and with fire." (Luke 3:16)* He not only anticipated the Lord's coming, but also prepared for and ushered in that divine visitation. He made "ready a people prepared for the Lord." (Luke 1:17) Why, though, was it critical that a people be prepared?

This word *"prepared"* in Greek is *kataskeuazo* which means to erect, build, prepare or make ready for use. It carries the connotation of being built or equipped with everything necessary to be used properly at the right time.

This term is used for the constructing of Noah's ark in 1 Peter 3:20, *"Who formerly were disobedient, when once the Divine longsuffering waited in the days of Noah, while the ark was being prepared (kataskeuazo), in which a few, that is, eight souls, were saved through water."* Due to the coming flood, an ark needed to be built for those who would survive. What would have happened during the flood if an ark had not been prepared? Who could have endured the pelting rain, mountainous waves, and deluges of judgment?

This verb is also used for the erecting of Moses' tabernacle in Hebrews 9:2-3, *"For a tabernacle was prepared (kataskeuazo): the first part, in which was the lampstand, the table, and the showbread, which is called the sanctuary; and behind the second veil, the part of the tabernacle which is called the Holiest of All."* Due to the coming glory, a tabernacle needed to be built to house His presence. What would have happened when His glory appeared if a tabernacle had not been prepared? Who could have endured His sheer, raw and fiery presence?

Whether an ark in Noah's day, a tabernacle in Moses' day, or the hearts of men in John the Baptist's day, preparation needed to happen in order for men to survive and even thrive in seasons of divine visitation. Unprepared people may not only miss the Lord, but actually oppose Him as well. To the extent that people were made ready by John, to that extent they embraced Jesus. To the extent that they were not made ready, to that extent they resisted Him. *"All the people, even the tax collectors, when they heard Jesus' words, acknowledged that God's way was right, because they had been baptized by John. But the Pharisees and experts in the law rejected God's purpose for themselves, because they had not been baptized by John."* (Luke 7:29–30 NIV[6])

If such preparation was necessary for the coming of Christ to the planet, would it not also be needed for the coming of the Spirit to our church, city or nation? Such readiness is as crucial now as it was then. So how did John prepare the people? In what way did he usher in this visitation?

In the Spirit and Power of Elijah

He will also go before Him in the spirit and power of Elijah… Luke 1:17

The angel Gabriel told Zacharias, John's father, that his son would go in the spirit and power *"of Elijah,"* but why Elijah? Why not in the spirit and power of Moses, David, Jeremiah or Daniel? Because in attitude, word and deed, Elijah's life uniquely shows us

6 *New International Version* (International Bible Society, 1973, 1978, 1984)

how to prepare the way of the Lord. Furthermore, his days uniquely show us the circumstances into which God chooses to intervene. Overall, Elijah's story is our example.[7] Specifically, though, the angel focuses on two aspects of his life to be imitated: his *"spirit"* and *"power."*

In regard to the spirit, this term can refer to the nature or essence of God, of a heavenly creature, or of the inward part of man. That which is spirit is invisible, higher-dimensional and otherworldly. Thus God *"is spirit" (John 4:24)*, makes *"His angels spirits" (Heb. 1:7)*, and formed men with a *"spirit, soul, and body." (1 Thess. 5:23)*

However, this word spirit can also refer to a person's disposition or attitude, not just his nature or essence. It can speak of one's character and inner moral compass. So in this way Paul uses the term when writing, *"Shall I come to you with a rod, or in love and a spirit of gentleness?" (1 Cor. 4:21)* Again, along these lines Paul declares, *"For God has not given us a spirit of fear, but of power and of love and of a sound mind." (2 Tim. 1:7)*

It is in this context that Gabriel speaks of the spirit of Elijah, for John was to imitate in every way Elijah's inner strength, rigorous honesty, character and attitude. Whatever made up Elijah's fearless inner disposition was to make up John's as well.

In regard to the power, this refers not to Elijah's character, but to his anointing. The Lord constantly worked through Elijah in prophetic, miraculous and supernatural ways. He was not just a preacher who spoke about God, but a prophet who spoke on God's behalf. He constantly and accurately foretold future events, disclosed hidden secrets, and performed signs and wonders. Again and again we read, *"Then the word of the Lord came to Elijah..." (1 Kings 17:2, 8; 18:1; 19:9; etc...)* In fact, there was such an abundance of

---

7 Jesus (Luke 4:25-26), Paul (Rom. 11:2-5) and James (James 5:16-18) depicted Elijah's life and circumstances as both instructive and applicable to their current situations. If this was true for the key leaders of the New Testament, it is certainly true for us as well.

supernatural activity in his life that the name *"the Lord, God of Elijah"* *(2 Kings 2:14)* was invoked when praying for miracles later on.

In the same way, John's ministry was not to be based on his eloquence or skills, but on the Spirit's anointing. So about his own ministry, John declared, *"A man can receive nothing unless it has been given to him from heaven." (John 3:27)* John's life was to be as heavenly and supernatural as Elijah's was.[8] Paul affirmed this same truth when he wrote, *"My message and my preaching were not with wise and persuasive words, but with a demonstration of the Spirit's power." (1 Cor. 2:4 NIV)*

Moreover, the order of this phrase in Luke 1:17 is important, for every detail in Scripture matters. We must first seek to walk in the spirit of Elijah, and then in his power. Great harm comes when people walk in a mighty anointing without having a strong character to sustain it. Consider the lives of Samson and Saul.

For John, anything less than a full imitating of Elijah's life would not have been sufficient to prepare the people for the Lord and turn the nation back to God. If that was true for John, is it not also true for us? The dark days of Ahab, Jezebel and Baal worship required a response like the prophet Elijah. The wicked days of Caesar, Herod and the Pharisees also required such a response. Do our days demand anything less?

We must remember that God always sends His brightest and most fiery prophets into the darkest and most evil periods of history. Zacharias made this point when he prophesied about his son John, for those were days of much wickedness. Into the days in which John was sent, men really dwelt *"in darkness and in the shadow of death." (Luke 1:79)*

If this is true, then the study of Elijah's life is crucial in this hour of history, and furthermore, God is going to emphasize Elijah as

---

8 Though this power in John's life did not result in miraculous works per se, it did result in the most impactful prophetic words ever given until that time. See Matt. 11:9-11 and John 10:41.

never before. In fact, such an emphasis is a sign of the times, for we are on the threshold of a historic outpouring of the Spirit followed by the return of the Son Himself. Speaking of the prophets and generations immediately preceding both the Lord's first and second comings, Malachi foretold, *"Behold, I will send you Elijah the prophet before the coming of the great and dreadful day of the Lord. And he will turn the hearts of the fathers to the children, and the hearts of the children to their fathers, lest I come and strike the earth with a curse." (Mal. 4:5-6)*[9] Before we delve further into this subject, though, I want to share how the Lord has highlighted these truths in my own life.

The Map Disclosed

As a young adolescent in the mid-eighties, one morning while sitting in our living room I was pondering Matthew 16:19, *"Whatever you bind on earth will be bound in heaven, and whatever you loose on earth will be loosed in heaven."* Then a few minutes later I started reading *A Table in the Wilderness*, a daily devotional by the famed Chinese author Watchman Nee. The text was Matthew 18:18, which is identical to 16:19, and regarding this verse he wrote: "In this the church should be heaven's outlet, the channel of release for heaven's power, the medium of accomplishment of God's purpose. Many things have accumulated in heaven because God has not yet found His outlet on earth; the church has not yet prayed."[10]

As I began to meditate on this, suddenly, in a heavenly vision I saw many immense storehouses. Each structure was like the size of an entire city. The Lord led me into a couple of them, and on numerous golden shelves I beheld a huge assortment of weapons, armor, tools, instruments, vessels, and other treasures. In these

---

9 According to Jesus' own commentary on Malachi 4:5-6 in Matthew 17:11-13, this prophecy was initially and partially fulfilled prior to His first coming, yet it will be finally and completely fulfilled just before His second coming. As with other Old Testament prophecies, this one also has a dual fulfillment.
10 Watchman Nee, *A Table in the Wilderness* (Wheaton: Tyndale House, 1989), February 13th selection

storehouses was the great accumulation of His blessings. In another place I observed what looked like mighty oceans of water held back by incredible floodgates. These seas were the great accumulation of His power. I thought of verses which speak of heaven's floodgates like Malachi 3:10, *"And see if I will not throw open the floodgates of heaven and pour out so much blessing that you will not have room enough for it."* As the vision came to a close, I understood that a time is coming when every storehouse and every floodgate will be flung open, and then it will increasingly be *"on earth as it is in heaven."* *(Matt. 6:10)*

Afterwards, I asked the Lord when this will happen, and He responded with two insights: Firstly, He announced that the "tears of His children" will be a sign of its nearness. Since then, I've come to interpret that as wholehearted repentance as described in Joel 2:12, *"Turn to Me with all your heart, with fasting, with weeping, and with mourning."* Secondly, He remarked that 1 Kings 18 is the map to that destination. Up until that day, I knew of the account of Elijah at Mount Carmel, but that story had no exceptional significance in my life. That would change. In the ensuing years since that vision, the Lord would highlight 1 Kings 18 like words on a projector.

While with Youth With A Mission in 1993, I joined a team of about ten Indians on an outreach in Kholapur, a prominent city in Southern India. Our aim was to start new house fellowships in a poorer section of that pervasively Hindu metropolis. Upon arriving there, we found and rented two rooms in a small housing compound surrounded by four large slums. In front of our door was a lovely courtyard with a white, open-air tent shaded by numerous palm trees swaying overhead. Our daily routine consisted of an hour of worship, an hour of prayer, and an hour of Bible study before lunch and then house-to-house evangelism in the afternoon. One morning as we sat inside the tent, I led the study with 1 Kings 18 as my text, and something occurred which I will never forget.

After introducing the teaching by sharing the floodgate vision, I proceeded to dissect the chapter. Suddenly and unexpectedly, the Lord's presence rested on me as I taught. My hands and arms literally began burning with a sensation of fire and electricity. It was not painful, but instead rather exhilarating. As with a hot iron, this experience burned this brand even deeper into my heart: the truth that 1 Kings 18 is the map to that destination.

The Message Confirmed

Ten years later in early 2003, like the lifting of a thick fog, the Lord brought to me considerable clarity about 1 Kings 18. Week after week I meditated on this chapter, read commentaries, developed outlines, and began typing out lessons. The words began to flow until I had written a ninety-four page manuscript entitled *The Spirit and Power of Elijah* replete with teachings on preparation, prayer, and repentance. This became part of the precursor to this present book.

As I neared the finishing touches of that writing, one afternoon I remember quietly sitting on our living room floor. It was a serene moment. The windows were open, and sunlight glistened in. A chorus of chirping birds and rustling leaves resonated all around. Barely above a whisper, I asked, "Lord, is this really true? Is this really going to happen? This preparing the way of the Lord? The forerunner mandate? The ministry of Elijah? The turning of hearts on a massive scale?"

Suddenly, I heard His voice. It wasn't audible to my physical ears, but still utterly unambiguous to my heart. He answered, "A day is coming when the sound of mourning will be more prevalent than the sound of singing in the church. A day is coming when the words of confession will be more prevalent than the words of preaching in the church." I was astonished, for I then realized that I still hardly understood the meaning of passages like 1 Kings 18, Joel 2, and

Malachi 4. How much does singing fill our sanctuaries? How much does preaching pervade our services? What would such a season look like…mourning, weeping, and confession on an unprecedented scale? The more I considered this prophetic word, the more I trembled inside.

I then asked the Lord for a sign, a confirmation, regarding this message. A couple of hours later while on the internet, I saw an announcement: "*The Return of the King* coming soon starring Elijah…" Reading on, I learned that Elijah Wood would be playing Frodo, the main character in the upcoming film *The Return of the King*, the third installment of *The Lord of the Rings* series. For me, this online declaration was more than just a passing coincidence, but a prophetic sign. Moreover, after having watched *The Return of the King* months later, I believe that this epic contains a prophetic message for the church in particular and the world in general.

Despite what the Lord had already established, further confirmations were granted. A couple of days later, one of our pastors phoned and asked if I would teach a Bible study for the Fall 2003 semester, and I responded that I would enjoy teaching through 1 Kings 18. So, one evening I started printing out my ninety-four page manuscript to glean notes for the upcoming class. My father-in-law, who also was on staff at the church at that time, walked by and asked what I was doing, and I told him that I was printing a book I wrote entitled *The Spirit and Power of Elijah*. Except for my wife, I had not told anyone about these teachings.

He then inquired if I had read the email our senior pastor sent out to the church staff a week previously. I didn't know what he was talking about, for I knew of no such email. He then proceeded to open up his inbox, find the email, and show it to me. I read it with utter astonishment.

Our head pastor wrote that while in prayer he had sensed the

Lord guiding him to pray for the spirit of Elijah to come upon the church. He then asked if any of his staff had any further thoughts or insights regarding this. This was especially remarkable as neither our church's leadership nor congregation used such language. Although not an intended recipient of that email, I forwarded to him my book and mentioned my elation at what the Spirit had spoken to him.

Two weeks later during our Sunday morning service, worship billowed forth from the congregation. As voices lifted in song, the Lord told me there would be a prophecy about Elijah that morning. I then asked if I was the one to speak this prophecy, but He said another would relay it. For our local fellowship, it had been the practice to share prophetic words after the praise and worship which lasted for about thirty minutes. As people sang, a nervous expectation welled up within me. Did I truly hear from the Lord? Would such a prophecy really be given?

Eventually, the music faded, and silence pervaded. Suddenly, a man stood up and forcefully prophesied. He recounted the story of 1 Kings 18, called us to follow Elijah's example, and foretold of the coming rain! At no time had our pastor told the congregation about his personally praying for the coming of the spirit of Elijah. Later on, I talked with the man who prophesied that Sunday morning, and he assured me that nobody had spoken to him beforehand about 1 Kings 18 or Elijah's ministry. It was truly another Spirit-initiated confirmation!

CHAPTER 4

NEITHER DEW NOR RAIN
(Sam Cerny)

There shall not be dew nor rain these years, except at my word.
1 Kings 17:1

God's Jealous Anger
Now Ahab the son of Omri did evil in the sight of the Lord, more than all who were before him...Ahab did more to provoke the Lord God of Israel to anger than all the kings of Israel who were before him. 1 Kings 16:30-33

Before we examine Elijah and the Mount Carmel confrontation in 1 Kings 18, we need to understand the events leading up to this time. In 930 B.C., a civil war erupted and split the Israeli nation between the northern kingdom and southern kingdoms. (1 Kings 11-12) Following that schism, a series of seven evil kings ruled the northern kingdom from 930 to 874, and each increasingly incited the Lord's anger. (12-16) Finally, in 874 Ahab ascended Israel's throne as the eighth since the division, and his wickedness surpassed all of his predecessors. To this, how would the Lord of love respond? Would He care? Would He be indifferent? Would He ignore their downward slide?

1 Kings 16:33 says, *"Ahab did more to provoke the Lord God of Israel to anger..."* This verb translated *"provoke to anger"* is ka'as meaning to agitate, stir up anger or grieve. "This term, when applied to God, implies that man can affect the very heart of God so as to cause him heat, pain, or grief to various degrees of intensity."[11] In other words, God was upset with Israel. To comprehend the ramifications of 1

---

11 Eds. R. Laird Harris, Gleason L. Archer, Jr., and Bruce K. Waltke, *Theological Wordbook of the Old Testament* (Chicago: Moody Press, 1980), vol. 1 p. 451

Kings 16:33, though, we need to understand this divine anger. The Lord's anger is not from Him being bad-tempered. These are not capricious, unpredictable outbursts of wrath, nor is His anger a result of some cruelness or meanness on His part. God is not like the ill-tempered fathers that many have grown up with. *"Every good gift and every perfect gift is from above, and comes down from the Father of lights, with whom there is no variation or shadow of turning." (James 1:17)*

God's anger burns from a heart that loves perfectly. Because people are so precious to God, He doesn't want to share them with idols and demons that would lead them to eternal torment. If a husband genuinely loves his wife, then he would be deeply jealous of any other lover who would attempt to seduce and hurt her. Thus God's fiery anger is simply an expression of His loving jealousy. *"They have provoked Me to jealousy by what is not God; they have moved Me to anger (ka'as) by their foolish idols." (Deut. 32:21) "For they provoked Him to anger (ka'as) with their high places, and moved Him to jealousy with their carved images." (Ps. 78:58)*

His anger and jealousy were not just expressed in the Old Testament, but in the New Testament as well. God's perfect passions have not and will not change over time. Of Jesus, we read, *"So when He had looked around at them with anger, being grieved by the hardness of their hearts…" (Mark 3:5)* To the church in Corinth, Paul wrote, *"Therefore, my beloved, flee from idolatry…You cannot partake of the Lord's table and of the table of demons. Or do we provoke the Lord to jealousy? Are we stronger than He?" (1 Cor. 10:14, 21-22)* Again, James warned the brethren, *"Adulterers and adulteresses! Do you not know that friendship with the world is enmity with God? Whoever therefore wants to be a friend of the world makes himself an enemy of God. Or do you think that the Scripture says in vain, 'The Spirit who dwells in us yearns jealously'?" (James 4:4-5)*

Moreover, if His anger cannot be provoked, then the cross would be unnecessary. For it was that anger that Jesus became the recipient of in our stead. The cross proved without a shadow of a doubt God's burning hatred toward sin. *"Yet it pleased the Lord to crush Him; He has put Him to grief. When You make His soul an offering for sin..." (Isa. 53:10)*[12]

Israel's Audacious Idolatry

Then he set up an altar for Baal (a Canaanite god) in the temple of Baal, which he had built in Samaria. And Ahab made a wooden image (an Asherah, a Canaanite goddess). 1 Kings 16:32-33

What did king Ahab and the nation of Israel do to provoke the Lord's anger and arouse His jealousy? They engaged in idolatry, which is the honoring of something or someone above the Lord. It is the offering of themselves to something or someone besides the Lord. It is misdirected worship.

Furthermore, idolatry fuels the demonization of a society. When idols are embraced, demons are empowered. As examples, see Deuteronomy 32:16-17, Psalm 106:36-38, 1 Corinthians 10:19-21 and Revelation 9:20-21.

Under Ahab, though, idolatry reached a new height in the nation, for he *"did more to provoke the Lord God of Israel to anger than all the kings of Israel who were before him." (1 Kings 16:33)* How, then, are we to understand this idolatry in Ahab's days? In what ways did it reach an unprecedented level in Israel?

Firstly, Ahab married *"Jezebel the daughter of Ethbaal, king of the Sidonians." (1 Kings 16:31)* Jezebel's father was not only the king

---

12 While Jesus bore God's wrath for everyone, only those who have faith in Jesus will receive the benefit of His sacrifice. Those who reject Christ and the cross remain under God's wrath. "He who believes in the Son has everlasting life; and he who does not believe the Son shall not see life, but the wrath of God abides on him." (John 3:36) Moreover, while those in Jesus are saved from eternal wrath, they may still experience temporal judgments and discipline from God. Out of love, the Father may use persecutions, hardships and other trials to further purify, sanctify and prepare the hearts of His children. See 1 Cor. 11:30-32, Heb. 12:3-11, 1 Pet. 4:17 and Rev. 3:19.

of Tyre and Sidon, but also a priest of a particular Baal cult from that region, and his daughter continued to promote that cultic activity.[13] By marrying her and making her his queen, Ahab not only tolerated Baal worship, but now officially sanctioned it as a state-promoted religion. In other words, by doing this Ahab was "officially instituting and propagating Baal worship throughout his kingdom."[14]

What the Israeli government did with the religion of Baal, the American government has done with the religions of Darwinian evolution and humanism. America, too, has its state-sponsored false religions.

Moreover, in regards to idolatry, it is first exhibited in the heart, not in an altar room with stone statues and burning incense. (Ezek. 14:3-4, 7) Thus expressions of lust for women or greed for things are idolatrous as well. In fact, if materialism is one's religion, then a shopping mall has the potential to be a place of more idolatry than a Buddhist temple in India or Thailand. *"Put to death, therefore, whatever belongs to your earthly nature: sexual immorality, impurity, lust, evil desires and greed, which is idolatry." (Col. 3:5 NIV)*

Secondly, the pinnacle of idolatry in Israel was the offering of their own children as sacrifices to these false gods. When we read that *"In his days Hiel of Bethel built Jericho. He laid its foundation with Abiram his firstborn, and with his youngest son Segub he set up its gates." (1 Kings 16:34)*, we are most likely reading of a practice where new buildings or properties were dedicated to the local deities through the sacrificing of one's children. The sacrificing of children as foundation offerings was a practice well-documented in the ancient Eastern world. Thus regarding the worship of the Canaanites, we read, *"They served their idols, which became a snare to them. They even*

---

13 The name Ethbaal literally means "with him is Baal." Regarding him, "the first century Jewish historian Josephus refers to Ethbaal as a king-priest who ruled Tyre and Sidon for 32 years." (NIV Study Bible, ed. Kenneth Barker (Grand Rapids: Zondervan, 1985), notes on 1 Kings 16:31)
14 R. D. Patterson and Hermann J. Austel, "1, 2 Kings," The Expositor's Bible Commentary, Vol. 4, ed. Frank E. Gaebelein (Grand Rapids: Zondervan, 1992), p. 136

sacrificed their sons and their daughters to demons, and shed innocent blood, the blood of their sons and daughters, whom they sacrificed to the idols of Canaan; and the land was polluted with blood." (Ps. 106:36-38)

The more you love someone, the more costly a gift you will give him or her. A new girlfriend might get flowers, but a fiancée will get a diamond ring. Yet what is more valuable than one's own child? Just how much did Israel love these false gods and hate the true God? Regarding idols, those who *"bow down to them"* and *"serve them"* are those who actually *"hate Me." (Exod. 20:5)*

Given this reality, in America abortion is simply a sign of the extent of idolatry in the land. With her religions of humanism and materialism, America's babies are being sacrificed on the altars of personal comfort and economic convenience. It is as much the shedding of innocent blood as in the days of Ahab and Jezebel.

For a city, state or nation, there is a moment when idolatry, the demonization of society and the shedding of innocent blood reach a point of critical mass. At that point, the anger of the Lord is not just stirred, but spent. Wrath and judgment are poured out. His love and justice demand it. In such moments, the normal course of life ends. Massive divine interruptions and interventions take place. As an Old Testament example, such a season was described by Ezekiel, *"You have become guilty because of the blood you have shed and have become defiled by the idols you have made. You have brought your days to a close, and the end of your years has come." (Ezek. 22:4 NIV)* As a New Testament example, Jesus also foretold such a time when He declared, *"Fill up, then, the measure of your father's guilt... That on you may come all the righteous blood shed on the earth...Assuredly, I say to you, all these things will come upon this generation...See! Your house is left to you desolate..." (Matt. 23:32-38)*

When Elijah stepped onto the scene, Israel had reached such a moment of crisis. So what did the Lord say through Elijah? How did God respond to Israel's idolatry and violence? What did He give to the nation?

The Lord's Loving Discipline

And Elijah the Tishbite, of the inhabitants of Gilead, said to Ahab, "As the LORD God of Israel lives, before whom I stand, there shall not be dew nor rain these years, except at my word." 1 Kings 17:1

In 1 Kings 17:1, we have the first mention of Elijah in Scripture. We do not know anything about his life prior to this verse, and that is key to understand. All the preparation that led him to this point was done in the hidden, secret place. We are prepared to the extent that we obey when nobody is looking. *"And your Father who sees in secret will reward you openly." (Matt. 6:6)*

The first prophecy Elijah ever gives is about an impending drought, which would be very severe. Even if it did not rain, an early morning dew would still rest on the desert floor. In this case, though, neither dew nor rain would descend. For an agrarian culture like Israel's, this would be devastating.

Moreover, Elijah did not just prophesy this drought, but also prayed for it. We should pray for that which is God's will, not just for that which feels good. *"Elijah was a man with a nature like ours, and he prayed earnestly that it would not rain; and it did not rain on the land for three years and six months." (James 5:17)*

Yet why would God send a drought to Israel? Why would their refusal to repent lead to a restraining of rain? Why would He destroy the environment and economy of their nation? His intent was not to destroy the people, but their pride! His aim was to strike down their reliance on themselves and their idols. *"Be careful, or you will be enticed to turn away and worship other gods and bow down to them. Then the LORD's anger will burn against you, and he will shut the heavens so that it will not rain and the ground will yield no produce…" (Deut. 11:16-17 NIV) "I will break down your stubborn pride and make the sky above you like iron and the ground beneath you like bronze. Your strength will be spent in vain, because your soil will not yield its crops, nor will the trees of the land yield their fruit." (Lev. 26:19-20 NIV)*

Such a drought forces people into a place where they cannot continue in their own strength. Over time, none of their ingenious farming techniques, irrigation plans or other efforts will avail them anything. Crops, herds, finances, security, prosperity and future plans will wither away under the searing sun. That people will be ushered into a place there they can do nothing apart from God, and that is His intent in judgment. Unless people are led to a place of humility, they will not repent. *"When I shut up heaven and there is no rain, or command the locusts to devour the land, or send pestilence among My people, if My people who are called by My name will humble themselves, and pray and seek My face, and turn from their wicked ways, then I will hear from heaven, and will forgive their sin and heal their land." (2 Chron. 7:13-14)*

If individuals or families or cities or nations persistently turn away from the Lord, then because He loves them, He may make life difficult for them. *"Blessed is the man you discipline, O Lord." (Ps. 94:12 NIV)* *"But when we are judged, we are chastened by the Lord." (1 Cor. 11:32)* *"For whom the Lord loves He chastens."(Heb. 12:6)*

Regarding this, Bruce Wilkinson in his book Secrets of the Vine writes, "Chastening is something you feel as emotional anxiety, frustration, or distress. What used to bring you joy now doesn't. Pressures increase at work, at home, in your health or finances."[15] Such pressure is from the Lord's hand resisting us in order that we might repent and turn to Him. It is His hand of love. *"As many as I love, I rebuke and chasten. Therefore be zealous and repent." (Rev. 3:19)*

His Heavy Hand

While in southern India with a team from Youth With A

---

15 Bruce Wilkinson, *Secrets of the Vine* (Sisters, OR: Multnomah Publishers, Inc., 2001), p. 46

Mission, we experienced His discipline firsthand. Fruitfulness seemed to abound during our outreach in the city of Kholapur. Within a few weeks, small gatherings in many homes had begun, and Indians young and old were being healed, delivered and saved. However, in the middle of our outreach, something went terribly wrong. Weakness and illness struck almost our entire team. Ministry times grew dry. Worship turned stale. The Spirit seemed absent. Despair lingered in the air.

After a few days, Ketho, our team leader, suspended all activities including home gatherings, street preaching, passing out tracts, church visits, etc... Not knowing what had happened to us, our leader exhorted us to do nothing but seek God's face and listen for His voice. We complied, and after two days, the Lord spoke.

On that third day at around noon, the sun's unbearable heat enfolded us. In that season in southern India, shade and even the slightest breeze were precious commodities. Walking into our room, I met a team member lying on the hard concrete floor, for we had no beds. He beckoned me to pray for him, for he said he was too weak to even move. He could not even get up from the floor. The whole situation seemed so strange.

I laid my hand on him and prayed, but feeling overwhelmingly ineffective, I stopped. A few minutes later I stepped outside and meandered over to some palm trees. Under their shade, I cried out to God. Intuitively, I knew that this was neither a demonic assault nor a natural illness. Then I had a brief vision of God's hand pressing against us and resisting us, as described in David's lament, *"For day and night your hand was heavy upon me; my strength was sapped as in the heat of summer." (Ps. 32:4 NIV)*

I suddenly realized what was occurring. Our ministry was going in the right direction, but our hearts were not! I recalled the story in 1 Samuel 4 where Israel's army engaged the Philistines with everything used against Jericho in Joshua's day – the ark of the covenant, the priests, the earth-shaking shout, etc... They employed the same successful method, but without the same successful result. Why? Because persistent sin was tolerated, and their worship was corrupted. God's presence had departed, and they were defeated. After I pondered 1 Samuel 4, the Spirit then made our own sins very apparent.

Within moments verses like Numbers 11:1-10, Joshua 7, 1 Samuel 2:17, Malachi 1:12-13, 1 Corinthians 11:17-30, and James 3:16 came to mind. We were treating our worship times as something common, as somewhat of a bore. We were incessantly complaining about our living conditions. Disunity and divisiveness were prevalent. Afterwards, I shared all of this with our leader, and he called for a special meeting that night. Under the flicker of the one light in our one-room concrete apartment, we gathered together, confessed our sins, and repented before the Lord. In response, the Lord's favor swiftly returned and remained for the rest of the outreach.

CHAPTER 5

RAVENS AND WIDOWS
(Sam Cerny)

Then the word of the Lord came to him saying, "Get away from here and turn eastward, and hide by the Brook Cherith… 1 Kings 17:2-3

The Prophet Elijah

And Elijah the Tishbite, of the inhabitants of Gilead, said to Ahab, "As the LORD God of Israel lives, before whom I stand, there shall not be dew nor rain these years, except at my word." 1 Kings 17:1

The name Elijah means "The Lord (Yah) is my God," and his name both defines his message and describes his ministry. The aim of his life was to show that Yahweh, not Baal, is God. *"If the Lord is God, follow Him; but if Baal, then follow him." (1 Kings 18:21) "Hear me, O Lord, hear me, that this people may know that You are the Lord God." (18:37) "Now when all the people saw it, they fell on their faces; and they said, 'The Lord, He is God! The Lord, He is God." (18:39)*

Being named Elijah, his entire life was set up to challenge the false religion of Baal. In other words, he was born for conflict with the ideologies and powers of darkness. This is also true for us. Spiritual war will be our way of life.

Being named Elijah, he had no other purpose than to show the world that the Lord is God. This is also true for us. Our only aim in life is to disclose to the world that Jesus is Lord. Anything outside of that goal really doesn't matter. Living with this singular focus will be our way of life.

Moreover, we need to view this drought in light of Elijah's purpose. It was not just judgment upon the people of Israel, but upon the gods of Canaan. "Why choose a drought? Why emphasize that Yahweh lives? Elijah determines to attack Baalism at its theological center. Baal worshippers believed that their storm god made rain..."[16] "Lord of Canaanite religion and seen in the thunderstorms, Baal was worshiped as the god who provided fertility."[17] Thus this drought was to display the power of God and the powerlessness of Baal, who was believed to be the god who rides storm-clouds and brings rain to water fields and produce crops. Throughout the Bible, false gods are judged before the people in the hope that the people might acknowledge the true God, turn to Him, and be saved.

Regarding the plagues upon Egypt during Moses' days, each specifically targeted an Egyptian deity. The Egyptians praised the gods of the Nile, and God turned it to blood. They honored Heka, a frog-like goddess, and God sent a plague of frogs. They revered Apis, the cow god, and God destroyed their cattle with disease. They worshiped Ra, the sun god, and God darkened the land. *"And against all the gods of Egypt I will execute judgment: I am the Lord." (Exod. 12:12)*

Regarding the judgments upon Philistia during Samuel's days, they targeted the Philistine gods. *"The ark of the God of Israel must not remain with us, for His hand is harsh toward us and Dagon our god." (1 Sam. 5:7) "Perhaps He will lighten His hand from you, from your gods, and from your land." (6:5)*

Regarding the judgments upon the Babylonian empire during Daniel's days, they targeted the Babylonian gods, particularly their chief deity Bel or Merodach. *"Say, 'Babylon is taken, Bel is shamed. Merodach is broken in pieces; her idols are humiliated, her images are broken in pieces.'" (Jer. 50:2) "I will punish Bel in Babylon, and I will bring out of his mouth what he has swallowed." (51:44) "Therefore behold, the days*

---

16 House, Paul R., "1, 2 Kings," The New American Commentary (Broadman & Holman Publishers, 1995), 1 Kings 17:1 selection
17 Brand, Chad; Draper, Charles; England, Archie, Holman Illustrated Bible Dictionary (Holman Bible Publishers, 2003), "Baal" selection

are coming that I will bring judgment on the carved images of Babylon." (51:47)

During Paul's days, God continued to target the false gods of the land. Regarding the impact of Paul's ministry in Ephesus, the idol-makers said, *"So not only is this trade of ours in danger of falling into disrepute, but also the temple of the great Goddess Diana may be despised and her magnificence destroyed, whom all Asia and the world worship."* (Acts 19:27)

Regarding the global judgments in the end-times as depicted in the book of Revelation, they too will target false gods and false messiahs. For example, *"Then the fifth angel poured out his bowl on the throne of the beast, and his kingdom became full of darkness; and they gnawed their tongues because of the pain."* (Rev. 16:10)

This principle of God judging the deities and delivering the people is seen throughout history, and He always does this through His prophetic people. So how was Elijah made ready for such mighty confrontations? How does God prepare His prophets and servants to contend against darkness over cities, states or nations? While chapter 18 describes God's public presentation of Elijah, chapter 17 depicts His private preparation of the prophet.

Prepared through Seclusion

Get away from here and turn eastward, and hide by the Brook Cherith, which flows into the Jordan…Arise, go to Zarephath, which belongs to Sidon, and dwell there. 1 Kings 17:3, 9

Immediately after declaring the coming drought, the Lord tells Elijah to hide inside of Israel by the Brook Cherith and then to hide outside of Israel in the region of Sidon. Why does God hide Elijah right after he gives his first prophecy? And why does the Lord keep him hidden for an extended period of time? Through Biblical and church history, why does God repeatedly conceal His prophets and servants?

47

In that, God was protecting Elijah. Ahab and Jezebel were searching far and wide for Elijah to kill him. *"As the LORD your God lives, there is no nation or kingdom where my master has not sent someone to hunt for you; and when they said, 'He is not here,' he took an oath from the kingdom or nation that they could not find you." (1 Kings 18:10)*

Furthermore, God was preparing Elijah. Chapter 17 is not just about his protection, but also about his preparation. Often it is in hiddenness that God develops His leaders. Joseph was enslaved in Potiphar's house and imprisoned in the Egyptian dungeon for about 13 years before becoming a ruler in the nation (Gen. 37:2, 41:46). Moses dwelt in the backside of the desert for 40 years before becoming a prophet and deliverer (Acts 7:30). David lived in the wilderness, in caves and in remote locations for about 12 years before being enthroned as king (2 Sam. 5:4). John the Baptist was hidden in the desert for about 27 to 29 years before entering into public ministry (Luke 1:80, 3:1-2). Jesus was in a carpenter's shop till His ministry began at 30 years of age (Mark 6:3, Luke 3:23). Paul was prepared in the regions of Arabia and Syria for 14 years before stepping out as an apostle (Gal. 2:1).

In hiddenness, the Lord's leaders learn to live before an audience of One. They learn to live for the will of God, not for the affirmations, approval or praise of others. They learn to live to please Him, not to try to gain a reputation or build a ministry for themselves. Instead of trying to *"be seen by men" (Matt. 6:5)*, they go into *"the secret place; and your Father who sees in secret will reward you openly." (6:6)*

In hiddenness, God tests our hearts to see whom we're trying to please, whether others, ourselves or Him. In Galatians 1:11-17, Paul discusses his first three years of seclusion in Arabia, and that discussion is introduced with a question in 1:10, *"Or do I seek to please men? For I still pleased men, I would not be a servant of Christ."* Again, in another epistle he writes, *"But as we have been approved by God to be entrusted with the gospel, even so we speak, not as pleasing men, but God who tests our hearts." (1 Thess. 2:4)*

On many occasions God has hidden me, and in those seasons He tested my heart and exposed desires for others' praise and approval. One such moment happened on August 16, 1998, while on a missions outreach in southwest China. Our team, my wife Brooke, and I boarded a double-decker bus which would take us from Kunming, the capital of Yunnan province, to Lijiang, which has been called the Venice of Asia. It is an ancient, stone-laden city erected by the Naxi people, and its thoroughfares are lined with lovely canals. Our aim in Lijiang was to pray strategically and connect with the very few Christians residing there.

As the bus meandered across the lush, green landscapes of that region, eventually the sun dipped below the horizon, and stars began flickering in the night sky. As I lay on the somewhat claustrophobic bed, from about nine to midnight I read a fascinating book which detailed the author's visionary encounter before the judgment seat of Christ. As the writer beheld that heavenly scene, he saw various esteemed Christians well-known in many history books. However, in conversing with him, some of these ministers disclosed their own self-centeredness, lack of sincere love, and other impure motives. While lying there with my flashlight and book, suddenly the Spirit revealed some polluted motives within my own heart.

Firstly, for days I had been desiring and praying for a video camera. I often imagined presenting a video of our outreach to friends and supporters back at home. Yet in that moment I perceived that behind this desire was a deeper desire for others to be impressed with me and my Asian adventures.

Secondly, earlier that day Brooke called her family back in California, and she heard that my close friend had spoken at a high school summer camp and made some remarks about our ministry in China. When Brooke relayed that to me, in my heart jealousy and competitiveness were ignited. I wanted to be the one to preach to the youth. I wanted to be the leader who was both esteemed and respected by those high schoolers.

Thirdly, during the past few days, I had been yearning for some visible, tangible results from my ministry. I longed to see signs, wonders, miracles, healings, and conversions. Why? Because I wanted exciting stories to share with others. Much to my dismay, however, in that season the Lord was keeping me in the prayer closet and hiding me from the eyes of men, and that was agitating my ego. As the bus rumbled along in the quietness of that late night hour, I confessed my self-centeredness and repented for my pride. The motives of my heart were laid bare before the Lord, and in that exposed place I was drawn closer and closer to my divine Lover. With James 4:6 in mind, I kept praying, "Lord, humble me. Grant me greater grace." Nothing produces intimacy like honesty and humility.

Lastly, when talking about seasons of hiddenness, I am talking about God leading us into obscurity, but not away from community. Even when our works seem unnoticed, we should still maintain close friendships with those around us. Even when our fruit is not apparent, we should still stay connected within a community of believers. Even when we feel overlooked, we should still honor and submit to the leaders God has put over us. In the caves, David still had his fellowship of mighty men. In the deserts, John the Baptist still had his community of disciples. We grow and develop in the context of relationships, not outside of them. *"Not forsaking the assembling of ourselves together, as is the manner of some, but exhorting one another." (Heb. 10:25)*

Prepared through Direction

Then the word of the Lord came to him, saying, "Get away from here and turn eastward…" Then the word of the Lord came to him, saying, "Arise, go to Zarepheth…" 1 Kings 17:2-3, 8-9

Elijah followed the Lord. His life was directed by God. He made minor and major decisions according to what the Lord said, not just according to his natural plans or personal ambitions.

This is a major key in our relationship with God. Our willingness to go where He leads is a sign that we are His, and not our own. Some don't experience God as Father because they refuse to be led as sons and daughters. *"The wind blows where it wishes, and you hear the sound of it, but cannot tell where it comes from and where it is going. So is everyone who is born of the Spirit." (John 3:8) "For as many are led by the Spirit of God, these are sons of God." (Rom. 8:14)*

Prepared through Provision

And it will be that you shall drink from the brook, and I have commanded the ravens to feed you there…See I have commanded a widow there to provide for you. 1 Kings 17:4, 9

Our trust in God is proven by our willingness to be provided for by God. We believe that He cares for us, but do we believe that He will show His care for us? Because He is a good Father, He will meet our needs in real and practical ways. *"Therefore do not worry, saying, 'What shall we eat?' or 'What shall we drink?' or 'What shall we wear?' For after all these things the Gentiles seek. For your heavenly Father knows that you need all these things. But seek first the kingdom of God and His righteousness, and all these things shall be added to you." (Matt. 6:31-33)*

In Elijah's story, not only do we see the Lord provide, but we learn how He provides. Chapter 17 is full of principles of divine provision for His people. Firstly, where God guides, He supplies. Take note of the word *"there"* in vs. 4 and 9. For when we are *"there"*

– in the place God has directed us to – then we can expect provision.

God provides in different ways at different times. For Elijah, one time sustenance came through ravens (1 Kings 17:4), another time through a poor, Gentile widow (17:9), and even later on through an angel (19:5). Jesus and His disciples received food miraculously multiplied (Mark 8:17-21), a coin from a fish's mouth for taxes (Matt. 17:24-27), and financial support through a group of women (Luke 8:2-3). Sometimes Paul earned money through making tents (Acts 18:3, 1 Thess. 2:9) and other times through offerings from churches (Phil. 4:14-19). In other words, receiving supernatural support is a matter of having faith, not following a formula.

God provides for people who give. From her last morsel of food, the widow was told to give a meal to Elijah first, and then to herself and her son. She complied, and her act of sacrificial generosity made way for God's act of substantial provision (1 Kings 17:9-16). Jesus summed up this principle when He taught, *"Give, and it will be given to you: good measure, pressed down, shaken together, and running over will be put into your bosom. For with the measure you use, it will be measured back to you." (Luke 6:38)*

God provides abundantly. He directed ravens to bring meat every morning and evening to Elijah (1 Kings 17:6). The common man in that era didn't eat meat every day, let alone twice a day. Kings, on the other hand, had meat daily at their tables (4:22-23). While the prophets of Baal ate at Queen Jezebel's table (18:19), Elijah ate at King Yahweh's table. He was provided for as a son of the King.

God's provision isn't affected by the world's economy. Even in the midst of a severe drought and famine where grains, grasses and livestock were perishing, His miraculous provision continued for Elijah. *"In times of disaster they will not wither; in days of famine they will enjoy plenty." (Ps. 37:19)*

Prepared through Determination

Then he cried out to the Lord and said, "O Lord my God, have You also brought tragedy on the widow with whom I lodge, by killing her son?" And he stretched himself out on the child three times, and cried out to the Lord and said, "O Lord my God, I pray, let this child's soul come back to him." (1 Kings 17:20-21)

As Elijah lived with the widow and her son in the region of Sidon, all three of them were supernaturally fed and kept alive during an unrelenting famine. However, at one point the son suddenly died from an illness. Why would God stop hunger, but not stop sickness? Why would He allow this to happen while Elijah was residing with them? Furthermore, the widow even blames Elijah for his death, for perhaps the prophet unleashed judgment upon them for their sins.

When God seems to be unjust, to not make sense or to disappoint us, how should we respond? When He seems to be far off, silent or ignoring us, what should we do? Many accept that as inevitable, give up and stop pursuing the Lord. However, Jesus taught his disciples a parable *"to show them that they should always pray and not give up." (Luke 18:1 NIV)*

How did Elijah respond to this tragic situation? He became even more determined for God to intervene and even more persistent in prayer. God will use trials to prepare us, and if we react rightly, those trials will produce in us perseverance. *"We also glory in tribulations, knowing that tribulation produces perseverance." (Rom. 5:3)*

To the extent that we do not give up, we will reach our destination. Thus determination, persistence and perseverance are necessary ingredients for fulfilling our ministries and callings. Because Elijah pressed through in prayer, the Lord raised the widow's son from the dead. Never before in recorded Biblical history had someone been raised from the dead. This was the first time! This trial became one of Elijah's greatest triumphs! *"Let us not become weary in doing good, for at the proper time we will reap a harvest if we do not give up." (Gal. 6:9 NIV)*

CHAPTER 6

LAYING DOWN YOUR LIFE
(Sam Cerny)

For so it was, while Jezebel massacred the prophets of the Lord... 1 Kings 18:4

Presenting Himself to Ahab

And it came to pass after many days that the word of the LORD came to Elijah, in the third year, saying, "Go, present yourself to Ahab, and I will send rain on the earth." So Elijah went to present himself to Ahab... 1 Kings 18:1-2

In chapter 18, every step Elijah took was in obedience to God's directives, for he said, *"I have done all these things at Your word." (1 Kings 18:36)* His obedience resulted in God sending fire from heaven, leading the people into repentance, having the prophets of Baal executed and ending the drought with a heavy rain. However, none of that would have happened if Elijah had not obeyed the initial command, *"Go, present yourself to Ahab." (18:1)*

To understand the seriousness of this command, we need to understand what it meant for a prophet of God to present himself to Ahab. The more people give themselves to idolatry, the more hostile they become toward Christianity. Both Biblical and church history bear witness to this fact. Thus Ahab and Jezebel did not just seek to promote the worship of Baal, but also to snuff out the worship of Yahweh. Ultimately, that meant silencing and even slaying the prophets and servants of the Lord.

As we shall see in the next few verses, presenting oneself to Ahab meant being willing to lay down one's reputation, freedom and even life. For genuine obedience to come forth in our lives, these same three issues need to be settled in our hearts. This was true for Elijah's days, for John the Baptist's days, and for our days as well.

Laying Down Your Reputation

Then it happened, when Ahab saw Elijah, that Ahab said to him, "Is that you, O troubler of Israel?" (1 Kings 18:17)

When you stand for the Lord and speak His words, your reputation may be ruined. For Elijah, his announcing of the drought was hugely misrepresented. At that time, the state-sponsored religion was the worship of Baal, and in Canaanite mythology, Baal was known as the god who rides upon the clouds, brings storms, and causes the fields to be fertile. In Canaanite literature, an epithet for Baal is "him who rides upon the clouds," and using divinely inspired sarcasm, King David declares in Psalm 68:4 that this title for Baal is to be ascribed to Yahweh alone: *"Sing to God, sing praise to his name, extol him who rides on the clouds - his name is the Lord (Yahweh)..." (NIV)* In light of this, Ahab most likely believed that Elijah's hostile attitude angered Baal thus causing this god to withhold rain from the land. So, in speaking the Lord's words, Elijah had to be willing to be misconstrued and slandered even by the king of the nation.

About how John the Baptist was viewed, Jesus commented, *"For John came neither eating nor drinking, and they say, 'He has a demon.'" (Matt. 11:18)* Why were the religious leaders and others so virulent toward John? His services were held out in the desert instead of within the religious system in the temple courts of Jerusalem. Also, his messages were *"speaking the truth in love" (Eph. 4:15)* and neither diplomatic nor politically correct. For example, *"Then he said to the multitudes that came out to be baptized by him, 'Brood of vipers! Who warned you to flee from the wrath to come?'" (Luke 3:7)* This was not a criticism, but simply a statement of fact. The people had given themselves to evil, were demonized and filled with snakes, and in need of real repentance. As a result of this, though, many who were offended said that it was John who opposed God's purposes and was

56

influenced by demons. Thus, to speak the truth in love, John had to be willing to be misrepresented and defamed.

About how we will be perceived, Jesus stated, *"If they have called the master of the house Beelzebub (the ruler of demons – Matt. 12:24), how much more will they call those of his household!" (Matt. 10:25)* Given this reality, we need to make it our aim to please God, not man. *"Am I now trying to win the approval of men, or of God? Or am I trying to please men? If I were still trying to please men, I would not be a servant of Christ. I want you to know, brothers, that the gospel I preached is not something that man made up." (Gal. 1:10-11 NIV)* In other words, we should say what God is saying, not simply what others want to hear. Often the truth is offensive or difficult to speak, but that is what we are called to speak. We too need to be willing to be misrepresented or defamed as we endeavor to proclaim God's Word.

Where do we learn to lay down our reputations? This is first learned with our family, friends and associates, and then later on with cities, nations and leaders. With those closest to us, our goal should be to speak the truth in love, not just words to win their approval. This is not done out of a place of arrogance (I'm right, and you're wrong), but out of a place of love (I really want what's best for you). Thus in many situations, trying to please someone is the opposite of loving them.

Laying Down Your Freedom

For so it was, while Jezebel massacred the prophets of the LORD, that Obadiah had taken one hundred prophets and hidden them, fifty to a cave, and had fed them with bread and water. 1 Kings 18:4

When you stand for the Lord and speak His words, you may lose your freedom. For many prophets in Elijah's day, they ended up hiding in caves from the murderous regime. Thus, as a result of proclaiming God's words, basic liberties were restricted like the freedom to walk down the road, to live with their families, to shop at the local markets and to interact with others publicly.

About John the Baptist, we read, *"But Herod the tetrarch, being rebuked by him concerning Herodias, his brother Philip's wife, and for all the evils which Herod had done, also added this, above all, that he shut John up in prison." (Luke 3:19-20)* He was imprisoned for speaking the truth, and all of his rights and freedoms were stripped from him.

This too will be the experience of many of us, for Jesus said, *"But when they arrest you, do not worry about what to say or how to say it. At that time you will be given what to say." (Matt. 10:19 NIV)* It is not a matter of if, but when we will be arrested for declaring the Lord's words.

Given this reality, we need to see that we are and will always be captives of Christ, and not of anyone else. As Paul sat in a prison in Rome around 60 A.D. (Eph. 6:20), he wrote to the Ephesian church. In that letter, did he call himself a prisoner of Rome or a captive of Caesar? No, he only called himself a *"prisoner of Jesus Christ" (Eph. 3:1)* and a *"prisoner of the Lord." (4:1)* Why? When we come to Christ, we become His, and He can spend us anyway He wants. In other words, when we say "yes" to Jesus, we lay down our rights and freedoms and take up His will. You are no longer yours. If He leads you into a stadium to preach or into a prison cell to suffer, either way you are His prisoner and should accept where He takes you.

On July 31, 1993, I arrived in Hong Kong ready to join a church planting team that would be moving to Lhasa, Tibet, later that summer. Our leader picked me up at the airport, and we drove to a retreat center high in the forested hills overlooking that vast Asian metropolis. The lush vegetation, spectacular views, and serene retreat grounds delighted my heart as I carried my luggage from the van to my sleeping quarters. Nevertheless, as I stepped through the doorway and into the tiny, whitewashed room, my heart sank.

Almost three years of constant transition bore down heavily

upon me, and I felt slightly depressed. My life's journey had become
a string of bland, whitewashed dorm or hotel rooms throughout
America, Israel, India, and now Hong Kong. That little room felt
suffocating to me, and I lamented to God that it felt like going from
prison to prison. He reminded me that Paul dealt with similar, but
actually much, much more severe circumstances: Prison to prison
in reality! That historical fact pierced my soul like an arrow, for Paul
really did spend a large portion of his life in dungeons, prison cells, or
under house arrest. The Lord then said, "You are Mine. I will spend
you as I will."

So where do we learn to give up our freedoms? This is learned
in the daily giving up of our own wants and needs. At times, this
means fasting instead of eating, watching and praying instead of
sleeping, giving away our money to the poor instead of spending it
on ourselves, singing in the Spirit instead of listening to the radio, or
helping a friend move his furniture instead of going to the movies.
Such steps prepare us for caves and prisons.

Laying Down Your Life

*For so it was, while Jezebel massacred the prophets of the Lord…And he
answered him, "It is I. Go, tell your master, 'Elijah is here.'" Then he said,
"How have I sinned, that you are delivering your servant into the hand of
Ahab, to kill me?" 1 Kings 18:4, 8-9*

When you stand for the Lord and speak His words, you may lose
your life. For many prophets in Elijah's day, their obedience led them
to their deaths. If they remained silent and compliant, they could
have lived, but they chose to obey instead.

For John the Baptist, his prophesying cost him his head. Because
he rebuked King Herod for having an affair with his brother's wife
and for other evils (Matt. 14:3-4, Luke 3:19-20), he was thrown into
prison. Eventually, Herod had the imprisoned prophet beheaded as
well. *"So he sent and had John beheaded in prison." (Matt. 14:10)* John

could have chosen to prophesy only "positive" words like announcing the blessings of the coming of Jesus and the Spirit, <u>but he was called to be obedient before God, not just positive before the world.</u> Thus he had to announce the coming of the Messiah and expose the sins of Herod.

For many of us as well, Jesus said that our obedience would lead to martyrdom. *"Now brother will deliver up brother to death, and a father his child; and children will rise up against parents and cause them to be put to death. And you will be hated by all for My name's sake…Then they will deliver you up to tribulation and kill you, and you will be hated by all nations for My name's sake." (Matt. 10:21-22, 24:9)* This is where we are headed.

In 1 Kings 18, God miraculously intervenes, but when did He intervene? This happened after the massacre of many prophets, not before. Why? Because martyrdom plays a crucial role in God's overall plan. The Psalmist declared, *"Precious in the sight of the Lord is the death of His saints." (Ps. 116:15)* This word *"precious"* is *yaqar*, which is from a root word meaning heavy, and it means weighty, costly or valuable. So martyrdom has a high value in God's estimation and agenda.

Given this reality, we need to see that we are already dead, and so in a sense, we cannot be killed. *"I have been crucified with Christ; it is no longer I who live, but Christ lives in me." (Gal. 2:20)* When you said "yes" to Christ, you joined Him on the cross. Your old nature with its selfish passions and sinful desires perished there, so you have no life outside of Him anymore. *"The life which I now live in the flesh I live by faith in the Son of God." (Gal. 2:20)* If they kill your body, it doesn't matter. As part of your old nature, your body too is fading away and perishing. That's why Jesus said, *"And do not fear those who kill the body…" (Matt. 10:28)*

So where do you learn to give up your life? Every day you dress

60

yourself, comb your hair, eat breakfast and brush your teeth. In the same way, remind yourself daily that you died with Christ on the cross and that your life is no longer about you, but about Him. *"Likewise you also, reckon (consider) yourselves to be dead indeed to sin, but alive to God in Christ Jesus our Lord." (Rom. 6:11)* This attitude will affect how you relate to God and others, for dead men cannot be driven by selfish ambition, offended, hurt or killed. Jesus called us to have this attitude daily. *"If anyone desires to come after Me, let him deny himself, and take up his cross daily, and follow Me. For whoever desires to save his life will lose it, but whoever loses his life for My sake will save it."* (Luke 9:23-24)

On many occasions the Lord has taught me to live for Him, regardless of my physical condition or outward circumstances. While living in Pune, India, in February 1993, I was hammered with an awful illness. At the beginning of this ordeal, my friend Jaap, a tall Dutch missionary, prayed for me and believed this would be a lesson from God. At that time, I was certainly not expecting everything that would entail.

The pain in my lower side and stomach area was unbearable, and hour after hour I laid on my bed crunched over in the fetal position. Wave after wave of agonizing discomfort crashed over me. A couple of days passed, and Ketho, one of the school leaders, finally took me to the local Seventh Day Adventist hospital.

A young doctor entered the room, prodded and poked my body, and asked numerous questions. He concluded that I suffered from appendicitis and that my appendix needed to be promptly extracted. He then stepped out of the room, and a nurse stepped in. With a large needle she shot a strong pain killer into my backside. They were preparing me for surgery.

After she departed, I looked at Ketho and begged him to find another doctor for a second opinion. He darted down the hallway and within minutes returned with an older physician, and this elderly gentleman told me to return home and drink lemon juice. Surgery or lemon juice? It took mere moments to choose the latter.

On the evening of the fourth day, a visiting minister conducted a class on power evangelism which I attended. Since the pain had not subsided, sitting through the long lecture was torturous. I remember being hunched over the desk and groaning in agony. After the teaching, he invited me forward, laid hands on me, and prayed for healing. Suddenly, the Spirit's power shot through my body like bolts of electricity, and I immediately collapsed to the floor. However, much to my chagrin, I was not completely healed until the following day.

On the night of that fifth day, having fully recovered I took a long walk down a dirt road amidst lush flowers, grasses, and trees. Along the way, I was troubled and asked the Lord, "If You knew You were going to heal me, then why wait for five days? Why allow me to suffer that long? Why not intervene sooner?"

In response to the continuous misery of the past few days, my heart had grown harder and more calloused towards Him. My lack of intimacy with the Lord suddenly became very apparent. He graciously responded, "Times of tremendous physical suffering are coming. You need to learn to keep spiritual communion regardless of your physical condition." In that moment, 2 Corinthians 4:16 came to mind: *"Therefore we do not lose heart. Though outwardly we are wasting away, yet inwardly we are being renewed day by day." (NIV)*

Lastly, it is in giving up your reputation, freedom and life that you gain true joy! This is the testimony of Scripture: *"Blessed are you when they revile and persecute you, and say all kinds of evil against you falsely for My sake. Rejoice and be exceedingly glad..." (Matt. 5:11-12) "And they agreed with him, and when they had called for the apostles and beaten them, they commanded that they should not speak in the name* of Jesus, and let them go. So they departed from the presence of the council, rejoicing that they were counted worthy to suffer shame for His name." (Acts 5:40-41) "Beloved, do not think it strange concerning the fiery trial which is to try you, as though some strange thing happened to you; but rejoice to the extent that you partake of Christ's sufferings..." (1 Pet. 4:12-13)

CHAPTER 7

FIRE ON THE ALTAR
(Sam Cerny)

Then the fire of the Lord fell and consumed the burnt sacrifice... 1 Kings 18:38

The Pattern of 1 Kings 18

And it came to pass after many days that the word of the LORD came to Elijah, in the third year, saying, "Go, present yourself to Ahab, and I will send rain on the earth."...Now it happened in the meantime that the sky became black with clouds and wind, and there was a heavy rain. 1 Kings 18:1, 45

As in the days of Elijah, sometimes there are droughts over cities, states and nations throughout the earth. Those could be physical droughts and famines from a lack of water (1 Kings 17:1, 2 Chron. 7:13, Rev. 6:5-6) or spiritual droughts from a lack of His spoken word and manifest presence (1 Sam. 3:1, Amos 8:11-12, Rev. 3:1).

In 1 Kings 18:1, Elijah prophesies that rain will be sent and the drought will be stopped, and at the end of the chapter in 18:45, a heavy rain does fall and the famine ends. So what happened between the prophecy and its fulfillment? What caused the word of the Lord to come to pass? What role did Elijah play in bringing in rain and breaking the drought? According the pattern of 1 Kings 18 and other Biblical passages, rain will follow repentance, repentance will follow His fire, and His fire will follow our prayers.

The Prayers of Elijah

Then you call on the name of your gods, and I will call on the name of the LORD; and the God who answers by fire, He is God...And it came to pass, at the time of the evening sacrifice, that Elijah the prophet came near and said, "Lord God…" Then the fire of the Lord fell… 1 Kings 18:24, 36, 38

Revivals, awakenings and transformations are not just God's activity, but His answers. They are not just the result of our efforts, but of our asking. Though God is all-sovereign and can do anything He chooses, He chooses to wait for our prayers.

Consider the role of prayer in the releasing of the fire of God's presence: *"Then the fire of the Lord fell…" (1 Kings 18:38)* What preceded this? Elijah praying. *"The prophet Elijah stepped forward and prayed…" (18:36 NIV)*

"Fire came down from heaven…the glory of the Lord filled the temple." (2 Chron. 7:1) What preceded this? Solomon praying. "Now when Solomon had finished praying…" (7:1)

"It filled the whole house where they were sitting. Then there appeared to them divided tongues, as of fire…" (Acts 2:2-3) What preceded this? The church praying. *"These all continued with one accord in prayer…" (1:14)*

Jesus laid out an irrefutable principle of His kingdom when He said, *"How much more will your heavenly Father give the Holy Spirit to those who ask Him!" (Luke 11:13)* In other words, He will not manifest His presence until His people pray. If this is true, then this unprecedented establishing of houses of prayer across the globe is a sign that an unprecedented unleashing of His manifest presence across the earth is coming. The sudden, dramatic increase of the prayer movement around this planet is a sign that this planet is being prepared for the fullest release of His Spirit and the return of His Son. Verses like Isaiah 56:7 and Malachi 1:11 prophesy not just churches, but praying churches in every nation, tribe and region of the earth.

In answer to Elijah's prayers, God sent fire from heaven. But what was this fire? What was the nature of these flames? What was the meaning of this blaze?

The Fire of the Lord

Then the fire of the LORD fell and consumed the burnt sacrifice, and the wood and the stones and the dust, and it licked up the water that was in the trench. 1 Kings 18:38

Not only did this fire fall from the sky, but the fire itself was unusual. Firstly, natural fire burns consumable materials like wood and animal sacrifices, yet this fire also devoured the rocks, dirt and many gallons of water. Not even the hardest stones could resist these heaven-sent flames, and all the consumable and non-consumable items were eaten up.

Secondly, this blaze was called the *"fire of the Lord."* (1 Kings 18:38) It was not merely natural fire from the Lord, but the supernatural fire of the Lord. Literally, it was the Lord's fire.

Thirdly, this phrase *"the fire of the Lord...consumed"* uses the Hebrew verb *akal* meaning to eat up, burn up, consume or devour. Throughout the Scriptures, this expression "consuming fire" or "devouring fire" often refers to the Lord's manifest presence. *"The sight of the glory of the Lord was like a consuming fire on top of the mountain in the eyes of the children of Israel."* (Exod. 24:17) *"Therefore understand today that the Lord your God is He who goes over before you as a consuming fire."* (Deut. 9:3) See also Psalm 50:3, Isaiah 30:30 and Hebrews 12:29.

Moreover, is the fire of the Lord merely intense heat, light and beauty, or something more? Besides grasping the nature of these flames, the Israelites also understood the meaning of these flames. About this, Moses said, *"Take heed to yourselves, lest you forget the covenant of the Lord your God which He made with you, and make for yourselves a carved image in the form of anything which the Lord your God has forbidden you. For the Lord your God is a consuming fire, a jealous God."* (Deut. 4:23-24) Along these same lines, Solomon declared, *"For love is as strong as death, its jealousy unyielding as the grave. It burns like blazing fire, like a mighty flame (lit. like the very flame of the Lord)." (Song of Solomon 8:6)*

This consuming fire is the burning of His jealousy, passion and love. His fire will burn away everything that opposes His will. It will consume everything that hinders His love. So throughout the Bible, these flames are described as purifying, refining and judging. *"Who can endure the day of His coming? And who can stand when He appears? For He is like a refiner's fire…" (Mal. 3:2)*

When encountering God's consuming fire, the humble will be convicted, cut to the heart, confess their sins and turn to the Lord. Such is their response when they really encounter His jealous love for them. As examples, see 1 Kings 18:38-39, Isaiah 6:4-7 and Acts 2:3, 37-38.

Furthermore, upon what did the fire fall? Where does God manifest His presence? The answer to that question is critical in this hour of history. These flames did not just descend upon any spot. They didn't just fall anywhere in Israel or upon Mount Carmel. No, the fire of the Lord falls upon one and only one place: the altar of the Lord.

The Altar of the Lord

Then with the stones he built at altar in the name of the Lord…And he put the wood in order, cut the bull in pieces, and laid it on the wood. 1 Kings 18:32-33

The sacrifice upon the altar depicted how God would approach man and how man should approach God. It symbolized the sin offering and the praise offering. Regarding the latter, throughout the New Testament, the altar sacrifice was the main illustration for true praise and worship: *"Therefore, I urge you, brothers, in view of God's mercy, to offer your bodies as living sacrifices, holy and pleasing to God – this is your spiritual act of worship." (Rom. 12:1 NIV)* See also Philippians

4:18, Hebrews 13:15 and 1 Peter 2:5.

How did a sacrifice upon an altar reveal true worship? In that Middle Eastern agrarian society, animals were of tremendous value. In their culture, owning animals was equivalent to owning cars, houses or bank accounts in our culture. However, once that flawless sheep or bull was laid upon the altar, it could no longer provide anything for its owner, neither clothing, food nor money if sold on the market. Its only purpose was to be *"a sweet aroma, an offering made by fire to the Lord." (Exod. 29:41)* In other words, true worship is that place where your life, time, money and energy are no longer for your pleasure, but for His pleasure.

Also, these verses in 1 King 18:30-35 don't just say that there was an altar and sacrifice, but they say how the altar was built and how the sacrifice was prepared. Every step Elijah took was directed by the Lord, for he said, *"And that I have done all these things at Your word." (1 Kings 18:36)* If we want God's fire to fall, then we need to follow this Biblical pattern.

Rebuilding Ruins
And he repaired the altar of the Lord that was broken down. 1 Kings 18:30

Elijah did not build a new altar, but rebuilt an old one. Why? These stones represented the devotion and worship of former generations, of his spiritual forefathers. Thus Elijah understood that God was not just responding to his sacrifice, but to the sacrifices of generations past. At that site, he was standing on spiritual foundations laid in prior generations, and he was building on those foundations.

The coming revival will be in response to prayers, tears and sacrifices from years, decades and even centuries past. So, these are not days to dig new wells per se, but to redig former wells which have been blocked up over time. *"Then the offering of Judah and Jerusalem will be pleasant (acceptable, pleasing) to the Lord, as in the days of old, as in*

69

former years." (Mal. 3:4)

Every work begun in former years, God will complete. Every promise given in days gone by, God will fulfill. Every prayer prayed according to His will in years past, God will answer. We need to remind Him of such things as Solomon did when he prayed, *"Therefore, Lord God of Israel, now keep what You promised Your servant David my father…And now, O Lord God of Israel, let Your word come true, which You have spoken to Your servant David." (2 Chron. 6:16-17)*

Restoring Unity

And Elijah took twelve stones, according to the number of the tribes of the sons of Jacob, to whom the word of the LORD had come, saying, "Israel shall be your name." Then with the stones he built an altar in the name of the LORD. 1 Kings 18:31-32

For almost one hundred years, the nation had been divided between Judah in the south and Israel in the north. However, Elijah's uniting of the twelve stones reveals that God never intended for this schism to happen. Through disobedience the tribes were severed, but this was never God's heart for them. "Selecting twelve stones according to the number of the tribes of Israel (a fact that underscored the divine displeasure concerning Jeroboam's schism), Elijah rebuilt the altar."[18] "The twelve stones were a practical declaration on the part of the prophet that the division of the nation into two kingdoms was at variance with the divine calling of Israel, inasmuch as according to the will of God the twelve tribes were to form one people of Jehovah."[19] Through reconstructing one altar with twelve stones, Elijah emphasized that God desires one people united, not many divided. This is not a statement against tribes being distinct, but against tribes not working together.

18 R. D. Patterson and Hermann J. Austel, "1, 2 Kings," *The Expositor's Bible Commentary*, Vol. 4, ed. Frank E. Gaebelein (Grand Rapids: Zondervan, 1992), p. 145
19 Keil and Delitzsch *Commentary On The Old Testament: New Updated Edition* (Hendrickson Publishers, Inc, 1996), Electronic Database, 1 Kings 18:31-35 selection

Furthermore, this was not just the uniting of twelve stones, but the uniting of twelve stones as an altar. God is not just seeking a people united, but a people united in worship. It is not enough just to be in unity, but we must seek to pray and praise in unison. It is one thing when a worshipper individually connects with the Lord, but quite another when a people corporately connect with Him. For this reason, Paul prayed, *"May the God who gives endurance and encouragement give you a spirit of unity among yourselves as you follow Christ Jesus, so that with one heart and mouth you may glorify the God and Father of our Lord Jesus Christ." (Rom 15:5-6 NIV)* Greater unity in prayer, worship and praise often leads to greater activity of the Spirit, for consider passages like 2 Chronicles 5:11-14 and Acts 4:24-31.

Why is it so important that we learn to serve, pray and worship in unity? Because to the extent that your heart is closed off to other people, your heart will be closed off to God. To the extent that your heart is open to others, your heart will be open to God. This is by the Lord's design. In other words, it is not possible to obey the first commandment without obeying the second as well (Matt. 22:37-40). About this, remember John's warning, *"If someone says, 'I love God,' and hates his brother, he is a liar; for he who does not love his brother whom he has seen, how can he love God whom he has not seen? And this commandment we have from Him: that he who loves God must love his brother also." (1 John 4:20-21)*

Acceptable Offerings
And he put the wood in order, cut the bull in pieces, and laid it on the wood. 1 Kings 18:31

When describing offerings of service and worship, the apostles constantly used adjectives like "acceptable" or "pleasing" as in the following verses: *"Present your bodies a living sacrifice, holy acceptable to God." (Rom. 12:1) "A sweet smelling aroma, an acceptable sacrifice, well pleasing to God." (Phil. 4:18) "But do not forget to do good and to share, for*

71

with such sacrifices God is well pleased." (Heb. 13:16)

By portraying certain offerings as pleasing to God, we can infer that other offerings are not so pleasing to Him. So what are the aspects of sacrifices acceptable to Him? Such offerings need to be presented through Jesus Christ (1 Pet. 2:5), motivated by love (1 Cor. 13:3), marked by generosity (Mark 12:41-44), infused with gratitude (Ps. 100:4) and offered without pride or pretense (Ps. 51:17).

However, 1 Kings 18:33 shows another facet of an acceptable sacrifice, and that is total surrender. When Moses showed Israel how to offer a pleasing offering, notice what he emphasized: *"He is to skin the burnt offering and cut it into pieces. The sons of Aaron the priest are to put fire on the altar and arrange wood on the fire. Then Aaron's sons the priests shall arrange the pieces, including the head and the fat, on the burning wood that is on the altar. He is to wash the inner parts and the legs with water, and the priest is to burn all of it on the altar. It is a burnt offering, an offering made by fire, an aroma pleasing to the LORD." (Lev. 1:6-9 NIV)*

The animal was to be offered piece by piece. Every part from the outer skin to the inner organs was cut up, laid on the altar and offered by fire. Following this process, Elijah also *"cut the bull in pieces, and laid it on the wood." (1 Kings 18:33)*

Why is there this emphasis on every part being distinctly offered? When we offer ourselves to God, we should offer all of ourselves. Just as the hidden pieces of the animal were exposed, the Lord will expose each hidden area of our lives and say, "Offer it." Every thought, every plan, every dream, every possession and everything else He entrusts in our care must be laid on the altar and sacrificed in worship.

The first time the word "worship" is used in the Bible is in Genesis 22:4-5, and often the first use of a word in Scripture defines that word from that point forward. *"Then on the third day Abraham lifted his eyes and saw the place afar off. And Abraham said to his young men, 'Stay here with the donkey; the lad and I will go yonder and worship, and we will come back to you.'" (Gen. 22:4-5)*

So how did Abraham worship? The Lord asked him to offer his son. *"Then He said, 'Take now your son, your only son Isaac, whom you love, and go to the land of Moriah, and offer him there as a burnt offering on one of the mountains of which I shall tell you.'" (Gen. 22:2)* Not only was Isaac the son loved by Abraham, but he was also the son through whom God would fulfill His promise to Abraham, a promise to give him descendants as the stars of the sky and through whom all the nations would be blessed. God was requiring Abraham to offer up what was seen – his son – and what was unseen – his hopes and dreams.

Abraham took that step of worship, bound his son and held up the knife to slay him. In that moment, how did the Lord respond? *"Because you have done this thing, and have not withheld your son, your only son, in blessing I will bless you..." (Gen. 22:16-17)* In other words, when God finds a people who withhold nothing from Him, then He will withhold nothing from them!

While living in Lhasa, the capital city of Tibet, a burden for the souls of Ngari, the westernmost province of that region, began to weigh heavily upon my heart. Missionaries were targeting different Tibet regions, but Ngari remained almost entirely overlooked. So, during the spring of 1994, my friend Jamie and I started planning a trip to Western Tibet to share the gospel, pray, and praise the Lord at key locations.

Using a local Tibetan travel agent in Lhasa, we began preparations for this summer endeavor. The entire expedition would require a month's time, and the journey would be arduous. The dirt roads across the plateau were rocky, muddy, icy, full of holes, and at times dangerous. Farther west the altitudes were higher and the weather even more unpredictable. A hot, sunny day could turn into a frigid hailstorm within an hour. Western travelers were rare, and much of that area was severely restricted by the Chinese Communist military.

Spiritually, this territory has been blanketed with darkness. In the heart of Ngari stands Mount Kailash, the most sacred spot in the universe for Buddhists and Hindus, and this region is renowned for its meditation caves, ancient Buddhist monasteries, countless pilgrims, and places of magical power. Many spiritual, political, and geographic obstacles abounded, but I was confident God would make a way.

Our plan was to travel there in a large transport truck, and our agent repeatedly said, "Yes, I will find you a truck. No problem. Don't worry, you will get a truck." However, weeks later I was told that it was illegal for foreigners to be transported in such trucks. In Tibet, the laws and restrictions for foreigners are innumerable!

So our travel agent tried to obtain a sport utility vehicle for us. Again, week after week he assured me, "Yes, I will find you a car. No problem. Don't worry, you will have a car." This too became seemingly impossible. Such vehicles only traveled to Ngari if accompanied by a large truck, for those trucks are needed to pull the cars out of any muddy ditches or deep rivers they get stuck in. Also, usually the larger truck carries the extensive amount of gasoline required. We could not afford both, though.

Finally, in early July I spoke with our agent about obtaining a vehicle, and he responded, "It's very difficult!" Because saying "No" is culturally inappropriate, "It's very difficult" is the Tibetan equivalent. With little time left, my hopes started fading like the setting sun. In mid-July my family arrived in Tibet for a ten-day vacation. Together we visited various farming villages, nomad encampments, sparkling lakes, and medieval monasteries. Near the end of our sojourn, we stopped in the southern city of Tsetang. At that time,

Jamie had already left America and arrived in Lhasa. I was to meet him in Lhasa in two days, and then the two of us were supposed to embark on our month-long journey. However, up until this point I still had heard nothing positive about our transportation.

Late one afternoon while sitting with my parents in their room in the Tsetang Hotel, I shared my predicament and felt anxious, angry, and hopeless. "Jamie has already arrived, my plans are set, and yet it seems like the bottom of this whole thing has fallen through!" I complained. My whole body was tense with frustration, and there was a harsh, edgy tone to my voice.

My mom gently replied, "The problem is that this has become your trip. You need to lay it on the altar before the Lord and surrender it back to Him. If it wasn't His trip in the first place, then let it die. If it is His, then He'll resurrect it." Even after her suggestion, though, I continued to complain.

However, that night I did take her advice, and at the side of my bed, I knelt down before the Lord, quietly prayed, and released this trip back to Him. I resolved in my heart that if this trip happened, it would be for Him, not for Jamie or me.

The next morning dawned, and yet hope was still elusive. There was still no news of any breakthrough regarding our transportation plight. Later that evening we were eating noodles in an outdoor restaurant. As we conversed back and forth, another driver sitting at a nearby table overheard us, leaned over, and remarked, "Are you the one looking for a car to go to Ngari? I heard that your agent found a Toyota Landcruiser and a driver able and willing to take you."

Sure enough, after arriving in Lhasa I met with a driver whose Landcruiser was owned by the Lhasa Holiday Inn, the most prestigious tourist establishment in Tibet at that time. Furthermore, he was one of the most experienced drivers in the country in traversing the regions of Western Tibet. Regarding carrying fuel, he was willing to tie down huge barrels of gas on the large overhead rack. In addition, the price he was charging was very reasonable. The Lord had wonderfully provided for us.

On July 22, we departed Lhasa early in the morning, and that day's drive was spectacular amidst snow-capped mountains, rushing waterfalls, lovely forests, golden barley fields, and little Tibetan stone villages which dotted the landscape. That afternoon we arrived in Shigatse, a large settlement on the shores of the mighty Yarlung Tsangpo River which winds its way through the Himalayan Mountains and eventually waters the Indian subcontinent as the Brahmaputra River.

After making hotel arrangements, Jamie and I did a prayer walk around Tashilumpo Monastery which sits on the side of a small mountain. As we neared the end of our hike, the golden, gilded-edged roofs of the various Buddhist temples within the monastery sparkled in the light of the setting sun.

After nightfall, in our hotel room we earnestly sought the Lord. While worshipping and praying, the Spirit emphasized Isaiah 64:7, *"And there is no one who calls on Your name, who stirs himself up to take hold of You."* This became the theme for our expedition - the pressing need to intercede for Western Tibet.

In that little room, suddenly the presence of the Lord rushed in like a raging fire. Under the weight of His glory, we lay down with our faces on the stone floor, and my hands literally burned as with fire and electricity. Adoration for Jesus poured out of our hearts, and that was the beginning of a remarkable month. The key to the success of that remarkable trip, though, was in the beginning when the Lord led me to an altar where I surrendered my plans, dreams and desires to Him. He needed to redirect my focus onto Him and off of my agenda, my reputation and myself. Upon such an altar God will send His fire.

CHAPTER 8

WHEN GOD TURNS HEARTS

(Sam Cerny)

And that You have turned their hearts back to You again. 1 Kings 18:37

The Unfolding of God

And it came to pass, at the time of the offering of the evening sacrifice, that Elijah the prophet came near and said, "...Hear me, O Lord, hear me, that this people may know that You are the Lord God..." 1 Kings 18:36-37

1 Kings 18 is a narrative of spiritual awakening on a national scale, and it was birthed in prayer. However, it is not just important that Elijah prayed, but also what he prayed. Elijah knew that what Israel needed most was not rain, fertile fields, a healthy economy or abundant blessings, but simply the Lord Himself. The main problem with Israel was not a drought, but their turning away from God. So he asks the Lord to release revelation of Himself and repentance toward Himself.

Thus Elijah's first request was *"let it be known this day that You are God in Israel"* and *"that this people may know that You are the Lord God."* *(1 Kings 18:36, 37)* To the extent that we know God, we will turn to Him. Without an accurate understanding of the Lord's nature, character and ways, people will not genuinely repent. *"Return to the Lord God, for He is..." (Joel 2:13)*

When we ask God to reveal Himself, how does He answer such a petition? How did He answer Elijah? A miraculous sign and wonder was given, which was fire falling from the sky to a stone altar on the earth. Signs are always meant to point to something. A sign on the freeway points to an upcoming city. A sign on the front of a building points to the business within. In the same way, signs from

God are meant to point people back to God.

So whether God sends fire from the sky, raises up a cripple, or turns water into wine, His intent in the miracle is to show Himself. Thus miracles are displays of His beauty which can capture the hearts of the people. *"This beginning of signs Jesus did in Cana of Galilee, and manifested (revealed, made known) His glory; and His disciples believed in Him." (John 2:11)*

The Gift of Repentance

...and that You have turned their hearts back to You again. 1 Kings 18:37

Elijah's second request is for the Lord to turn the hearts of the people back to Himself. In other words, he is asking the Lord to initiate repentance, and to repent simply means to turn to God and away from sin.

At its core, repentance is a change, not a feeling. It is not just feeling sorry for our sins, nor it is just weeping during an altar call at the end of a church service. It is a tangible change in our attitudes, words and deeds. True repentance has noticeable results. *"Therefore bear fruits worthy of repentance." (Matt. 3:8)*

However, in our own willpower we cannot turn to God as He demands. In our own strength we cannot turn away from sin as He requires. In and of ourselves, we cannot change as we ought to. Elijah understood this, and so he asked God to produce this repentance. He asked the Lord to turn their hearts. If we sincerely and humbly ask Him, He will do for us what we cannot do for ourselves. *"If God perhaps will grant them repentance, so that they may know the truth, and that they may come to their senses and escape the snare of the devil, having been taken captive by him to do his will." (2 Tim. 2:25-26)*

Many in the church comprehend God's gift of forgiveness, but they don't understand His gift of repentance. Both come from Him and both need to be received. *"Him God has exalted to His right hand to be Prince and Savior, to give repentance to Israel and forgiveness of sin." (Acts 5:31)*

great intercessory prayer scripture

Moreover, why does Elijah use the verb *"turned"* in 1 Kings 18:37 in the past tense? Had this repentance already happened, even prior to God's fire falling upon the altar? Many prayers and prophecies in the Bible are proleptic, which means to declare something which is still to happen in the future as having already happened. For example, in Romans 8:30 Paul says that God's people are *"glorified"* in the past tense. In the context of this chapter, though, such glorification clearly involves the resurrecting and regenerating of our bodies, which is unmistakably a future act as seen in 8:17-23.

So why does Paul use such a proleptic statement in Romans 8:30? Why does Elijah use one in 1 Kings 18:37? Each was so sure that it would happen, that he spoke as if it already happened. It is a way of declaring something with absolute certainty and confidence as to its outcome. Paul had no doubt that God was going to glorify the bodies of His people along with their spirits. Elijah had no doubt that God would turn the hearts of Israel back to Himself. He was certain of it.

The Heart of the Matter

...and that You have turned their hearts back to You again. 1 Kings 18:37

Notice that Elijah doesn't just ask God to turn the people, but specifically *"their hearts."* Why is that distinction crucial to grasp? Biblically, a person's heart is the seat of his intentions, attitudes and emotions. Moreover, our outward lives are determined by the condition of our inward hearts, just like a car will only drive as well as the condition of its engine under the hood. So Solomon said, *"Keep your heart with all diligence, for out of it spring the issues of life."* (Prov. 4:23)

Your heart is that secret, hidden place that only God sees. It is the underlying motivation for looking at that person of the opposite gender. It is the real reason behind sharing that "prayer request" about the pastor. It is the driving force behind what we say or do,

79

whether publicly or privately when nobody is looking. *"For man looks at the outward appearance, but the Lord looks at the heart." (1 Sam. 16:7)*

Overall, your heart is the place where you really meet or miss God, for Jesus said, *"Blessed are the pure in heart, for they will see God." (Matt. 5:8)* That is why repentance, or the turning of your heart, is so critical. You can pray, praise, fast, study the Scriptures, evangelize, serve others and feed the poor, but still not truly change from the inside out. You can do all of these things and still harbor pride, lust, resentment or unbelief. You can work all of these works and still resist God in your heart. *"Today, if you will hear His voice, do not harden your hearts." (Heb. 4:7)* Do not become offended by His word.

What shuts a person's heart off from the Lord? Not the 95% where he is obeying God, but the 5% where he is resisting Him. Not the 90% where he is saying, "Yes, Lord," but the 10% where he is insisting, "No, Lord!"

"I pray, read the Bible, go to church and serve in my home fellowship group, but I just need a little 'lust' time on the internet each week."

"I speak well of everyone at my church, except whenever I talk about that one certain pastor."

"I've forgiven everyone who has belittled me, but I won't forgive my husband."

"I've surrendered every part of my life to the Lord, but I just can't and won't tithe my money."

In all of these cases, that one area of resistance can shut off the entire heart. Thus it is that one unresponsive, unsurrendered area that the Lord will put His firm yet gentle finger on! We must come to God on His terms, not on ours.

For this reason, the Biblical injunction is not just to turn to God with our hearts, but with all of our hearts. *"Then Samuel spoke to all the house of Israel, saying, 'If you return to the Lord with all your hearts...'"*

(1 Sam. 7:3) *"And you will seek Me and find Me, when you search for Me with all your heart."* (Jer. 29:13) *"'Now, therefore,' says the Lord, 'Turn to me with all your heart...'"* (Joel 2:12) *"And you shall love the Lord your God with all your heart..."* (Mark 12:30)

In light of this, consider what is prophesied in Joel 2 and Malachi 3-4, which parallel each other in numerous ways. Both describe the days just prior to the Lord's second coming, for these are the only two passages in the Bible that have the phrase: *"Before the coming of the great and terrible (or dreadful) day of the Lord."* (Joel 2:31, Mal. 4:5)

Yet what is to occur in that final period? What is prophesied in these passages? Firstly, a prophetic ministry patterned after Elijah will once again step upon the scene. (Joel 2:28-29, Mal. 3:1, 4:5)

Secondly, that prophetic ministry will be marked by signs and wonders like miraculous fire from heaven (Joel 2:30, Mal. 3:2, 4:1) and the opening of the floodgates and pouring out of rain and blessings upon drought-stricken lands (Joel 2:23-24, Mal. 3:10-11).

Thirdly, at the core of these prophecies is a release of God-initiated repentance, the turning of hearts, on a massive scale! In fact, at the root of each of these prophecies is the language of Elijah's prayer for repentance in 1 Kings 18:37. Such wide-scale repentance will be a sign that we stand on the threshold of the end-times. *"For the day of the Lord is great and very terrible; who can endure it? 'Now, therefore,' says the Lord, 'Turn to Me with all your heart...'"* (Joel 2:11-12) *"Behold, I will send you Elijah the prophet before the coming of the great and dreadful day of the Lord. And he will turn the hearts..."* (Mal. 4:5-6) [20]

---

20 When Malachi prophecies that Elijah will "turn the hearts of the fathers to the children, and the hearts of the children to their fathers," he is not just talking about repentance in the context of restoring broken families, but also restoring broken generations. In his commentary on this verse, the angel Gabriel said that John, who initially and partially fulfilled it, would "turn many of the children of Israel to the Lord their God." (Luke 1:16) Yet how would that take place? What is the path to such large-scale, corporate repentance? The angel then quotes Mal. 4:6 and adds that John will turn "the disobedient to the wisdom of the just." (1:17) In other words, to turn to God, this wayward generation needs to turn back to the godly wisdom and spiritual foundations of former generations. They need to learn from and walk in the footsteps of their spiritual forefathers as detailed in both the Bible and in church history. Those before us have already forged the path for us. Examples of such a turning can be seen in Isa. 51:1-2, Jer. 6:16, and other passages.

Overall, what are Joel 2 and Malachi 3-4 prophesying? That 1 Kings 18 will happen again, but this time on a much, much larger scale!

The Pain and Joy of Repentance

Now when all the people saw it, they fell on their faces; and they said, "The Lord, He is God! The Lord, He is God!" And Elijah said to them, "Seize the prophets of Baal! Do not let one of them escape!" So they seized them; and Elijah brought them down to the Brooke Kishon and executed them there. (1 Kings 18:39-40)

In regard to these executions, Elijah and the Israelites were carrying out the death penalty enacted by the Law. Under the Old Testament stipulations, if false prophets tried to steer people into false, idolatrous worship, then they were to be slain. *"But that prophet or that dreamer of dreams shall be put to death, because he has spoken in order to turn you away from the Lord your God...to entice you from the way in which the Lord your God commanded you to walk." (Deut. 13:5)*

However, in 1 Kings 18:39-40 this was not just an act of law enforcement, but also of heart repentance. There is a seduction in idolatry that woos people into its clutches. Like a drug or quick fix, idolatry is used as a means to cope with life's problems, stresses, disappointments and resentments. Laying offerings at statues' feet, burning incense, repeating chants, seeking out soothsayers, receiving good fortunes or engaging in other cultic activities is intended to invoke a "god," pacify him and prevent life's troubles. Along these lines, the Israelites said to Jeremiah, *"But we will certainly do whatever has gone out of our own mouth, to burn incense to the queen of heaven and pour out drink offerings to her, as we have done, we and our fathers, our kings and our princes, in the cities of Judah and in the streets of Jerusalem. For then we had plenty of food, were well-off, and saw no trouble." (Jer. 44:17)*

Presently, in the western world the worship of statues may not be prevalent, but idolatry still is. Other things besides the Lord are sought after to cope with life's difficulties, and what kind of "idols" are pursued for such quick fixes? Perhaps drugs, alcohol, affairs, pornography, incessant television watching, obsessive video game playing, occult practices, the hoarding of material possessions, the selfish pursuit of status and success or other addictive behaviors. *"For this you know, that no fornicator, unclean person, nor covetous man, who is an idolater..." (Eph. 5:5)*

Regardless of what it is, when a person severs such things from his or her life, a measure of pain and loss may result for a time. However, if that momentary pain is avoided, that repentance will also be fleeting.

In putting to death the prophets of Baal, the Israelites were also putting to death their reliance on those prophets. No longer could they run to those soothsayers for predictions of good fortunes. No longer could they attempt to escape life's rigors by fleeing to Baal's shrines. Unlike with those idols, with God we face suffering rather than avoid it. With God we confess our sins rather than hide them. With God there are no quick fixes like the world chases after, but there is a loving Comforter and Healer.

Often repentance initially requires painful decisions. Some, though, are unwilling to make those decisions, and thus are unwilling to repent. They stand like the rich, young ruler who refused to follow Jesus because he refused to give up the riches which his heart was so bound to. Such surrender was simply too painful for him. *"But he was sad at this word, and went away grieved, for he had great possessions."* (Mark 10:22)

As stated in Joel 2:12-13, we are called to both *"turn"* and *"rend"* This word *"rend"* in Hebrew is *qara* meaning to tear away or split asunder. It is a forceful, violent and even painful term. The Lord will not allow us to hold onto Him with one hand and onto idols and sin with the other. He requires that we cling to Him and cut such

83

sin out of our lives. Along these same lines, Jesus said, *"If your right eye causes you to sin, pluck it out and cast it from you...And if your right hand causes you to sin, cut it off and cast it from you..."* (Matt. 5:29-30)

One afternoon many years ago, I was climbing up a steep mountainside near Big Bear, California. Being a hot summer day, a cloud of heat and dust swirled around me. Pine trees overhead swayed back and forth as wind gusts blew by. My destination was a tall rock outcropping piercing the dense trees on the ridge high above. From the top of those rocks would be a spectacular view of the landscape in every direction. No trail was carved out, so I was straining my way through thick underbrush, webs of pine branches, and over piles of rocks. Nevertheless, even with nature's tranquility surrounding me, peace eluded me.

That whole day I was deeply disturbed. For many years I had some nagging sins which I could not shake off despite my best efforts. Every few weeks or months, these sins would show their ugly head, and I would respond with every "right" action. During church altar calls I went forward to confess and receive prayer. With different friends I remained accountable, and together we walked in honesty. At times I made commitments and vows before the Lord accompanied by seasons of prayer and fasting. During some periods I consumed much Scripture in the spirit of Psalm 119:9, "How can a young man keep his way pure? By living according to your word." All of these actions helped, but not in an enduring way.

So, ascending the mountain that afternoon, I reached a place of complete desperation. Gazing into the vibrantly blue sky, I cried out, "Oh God, please help me. How can I finally stop these sin patterns? What steps must I take?" I had prayed this before, yet perhaps not with a total willingness to obey whatever He commanded.

Suddenly, like lightning striking, Matthew 5:29-30 came to mind. *"If your right eye causes you to sin, gouge it out and throw it away.*

It is better for you to lose one part of your body than for your whole body to be thrown into hell. And if your right hand causes you to sin, cut it off and throw it away. It is better for you to lose one part of your body than for your whole body to go into hell." (Matt. 5:29-30 NIV) Many times I had heard sermons about this passage, and most of them had the same point: We must deal ruthlessly with sin and cut it out of our lives entirely. Half-hearted measures do not count, but only wholehearted commitments. To me, these teachings spoke of the white-knuckle approach against sin. If only more committed, more determined and more faithful, we would walk in purity. Perhaps some could stand sin's assault, but I could not. Such sermons just left me in further despair. I just did not understand Matthew 5:29-30, and so I asked the Lord, "What do these verses really mean?"

He replied, "If you literally gouged out your eye, what is the one thing you would feel?"

"Pain, incredible pain," I answered.

"If you literally cut off your hand, what would you feel?"

"Pain. A lot of pain." I thought of the ferocious pain in actually cutting out an eye or chopping off a hand. That thought sent shivers through me.

"That is the meaning of this passage. If you are really going to stop this sin, you need to be willing to make those painful decisions." Instantly, the Spirit exposed my heart, and I knew what He was talking about. For years I had always confessed that I was a person "struggling" with this or that sin, but I refused to acknowledge that I was addicted. I was too proud to admit the latter. I considered myself a normal person battling sin, not an addict trapped in sin. Facing my utter depravity was simply too grievous. The devastating of my pride would be too painful, yet God required this very thing. My reputation, my errant belief that I was a "good" Christian with a few hang-ups, would have to die.

By this point, I arrived at the top of the mountain's ridge. Traversing over to the huge boulders, I climbed up until I discovered a flat place to sit. A vast array of forests, mountains, and deserts filled my view. At that moment, I knew what He was requesting of me.

A couple of days later, during my lunch break at work, I picked up the phone and called my pastor. I confessed, "I'm addicted. I'm caught in this sin and can't get free. I need Galatians 6:1 in my life." That was one of the most difficult steps I have ever taken. We conversed for about thirty minutes, and the wisdom he shared was invaluable. Over the next weeks, months, and years, I followed his recommendations and stepped into genuine repentance and restoration.

CHAPTER 9

OPENING THE FLOODGATES
(Sam Cerny)

Now it happened in the meantime that the sky became black with clouds and wind, and there was a heavy rain. 1 Kings 18:45

Transformation Far and Wide

In fulfillment of Elijah's prophecies and in answer to his prayers, fire falls, many turn back to the Lord, and the worship of Baal ⟵ suffers a severe blow. So how did this affect the nation and impact the people? What resulted from Elijah's ministry? What followed this Mount Carmel confrontation? Justice, righteousness and transformation spread throughout society and across generations.

The Lord's transforming work is not to be confined within the church, but rather to expand throughout the world. It is to pervade every facet of society and every aspect of culture. Everything is to be impacted by Him, from physical environments to educational systems to governmental seats.[21] Because this is God's intent, Paul told the church, *"Therefore I exhort first of all that supplications, prayers, intercessions, and giving of thanks be made for all men, for kings and all who are in authority..." (1 Tim. 2:1-2)*

Moreover, God's transforming activity is not to be contained within a generation, but rather to extend across the generations. What is started with fathers is to be fulfilled in their children. This is by God's design, for His purposes are never accomplished with just

---

21 In this age this God-initiated transformation is incremental and partial, yet in the age to come it will be complete and perfect. The Bible clearly says that both righteousness and wickedness will increase in the earth until the Lord's return (Matt. 13:24-43). However, to an extent, the prayers, repentance and obedience of the people can determine the measure of godly transformation experienced in a city, region or nation. This principle in passages like 2 Chron. 7:14 and Joel 2:12-19 has never changed.

an individual or a group, but rather through multiple generations. The Scriptures are replete with such examples. Promises conveyed to Abraham were carried on through Isaac, Jacob and their descendants. The promise of land given to Moses was realized through his spiritual son Joshua. The promise of a temple granted to David was fulfilled through his biological son Solomon. *"Which He commanded our fathers, that they should make them known to their children; that the generation to come might know them, the children who would be born, that they may arise and declare them to their children..." (Ps. 78:5-6)*

Why does the Lord work generationally? Because in this, He discloses and expresses His fatherhood and sonship through His people. As God relates within His triune self as Father, Son, and Holy Spirit, so we are to relate with each other from generation to generation. This aspect further unveils how we are made in His image. *"So God created man in His own image; in the image of God He created them... Then God blessed them, and God said to them, 'Be fruitful (with children) and multiply (generationally)...'" (Gen. 1:27-28)*

In light of this, we are not just called to obey God's commands for ourselves, but also to father and mother His children. That could include being biological or spiritual parents. We are to pass on to the next generation everything we have received, learned or experienced from the Lord. Consider the impact that Timothy's biological mother Eunice and spiritual father Paul had on his life: *"When I call to remembrance the genuine faith that is in you, which dwelt first in your grandmother Lois and your mother Eunice, and I am persuaded is in you also. Therefore I remind you to stir up the gift of God which is in you through the laying on of my hands." (2 Tim. 1:5-6)*

So how were the spheres of society affected by Elijah's ministry? How were the subsequent generations altered by His life? Seismic shifts occurred in the environmental, political and religious arenas of Israel and the surrounding nations.

Lands Replenished

Then Elijah said to Ahab, "Go up, eat and drink; for there is the sound of abundance of rain." (1 Kings 18:41)

In regard to environmental transformation, the seemingly never-ending drought and famine finally ended. With the fall of the prophets of Baal, Elijah immediately hears *"the sound of abundance of rain." (1 Kings 18:41)* This was not a natural sound, but a supernatural one. At this point, the sky was utterly clear and cloudless. Not a single raincloud could be seen, not even to the farthest horizon.

Elijah heard that prophetic sound of rain, and because of that sound, he entered into intense, fervent and persistent prayer. Six times he prayed and sent his servant to the top of the mountain to scan the sky for clouds, and six times the servant returned saying, *"There is nothing." (1 Kings 18:43)* Many do not see answers not because they don't pray, but because they don't pray persistently. Elijah understood this principle and refused to give up.

The seventh time, a tiny cloud appeared as small as a man's hand. After seeing that mere white spot in the sky, Elijah switches from prayer to preparation, for the land was about to be inundated with rain (1 Kings 18:44-45).

Finally, the rains plummeted down, and the drought was over. The environment and economy of Israel were suddenly and dramatically rejuvenated. Yet how was the drought broken? In what way did God replenish Israel's farms and lands?

When God ended the drought, He did not just use a few scattered showers. He did not simply release a light rain to start re-watering the land. No, He opened wide the floodgates of heaven, and a mighty downpour followed. The storm clouds gathered so thickly that *"the sky became black,"* and the rain fell so abundantly that it was *"a heavy rain." (1 Kings 18:45)*

This Hebrew word translated as *"heavy"* is *gadol* meaning great or large in magnitude, extent, number or intensity. When the Lord performs a work in the earth, often this adjective gadol describes it. *"Indeed seven years of great (gadol) plenty will come throughout all the land of Egypt." (Gen. 41:29) "Thus Israel saw the great (gadol) work which the Lord had done in Egypt." (Exod. 14:31) "But the Lord thundered with a loud (gadol) thunder upon the Philistines that day." (1 Sam. 7:10) "So I prophesied as He commanded me, and breath came into them, and they lived, and stood upon their feet, an exceedingly great (gadol) army." (Ezek. 37:10) "Before the coming of the great (gadol) and terrible day of the Lord." (Joel 2:31) "The glory of this latter temple shall be greater (gadol) than the former." (Hag. 2:9)*

Gadol speaks of prayers answered, prophecies fulfilled and works performed that will far surpass our expectations. In quality and quantity, God will do much more than we have ever hoped for. Overwhelmed with this thought, Paul exclaimed, *"Now to Him who is able to do exceedingly abundantly above all that we ask or think, according to the power that works in us." (Eph. 3:20)* However, the Lord did not just stop with this glorious environmental and economic shift, but He also sparked an amazing governmental and religious transformation in Israel.

Kings Raised Up

Then the Lord said to him: "Go, return on your way to the Wilderness of Damascus; and when you arrive, anoint Hazael as king over Syria. Also you shall anoint Jehu son of Nimshi as king over Israel." 1 Kings 19:15–16

Following the confrontation with Baal on Mt. Carmel, Elijah headed into an encounter with God on Mt. Horeb, which is another name for Mt. Sinai. That was the mountain where Moses fasted forty days and nights, faced God and received a divine commissioning for him and the Israeli nation (Exod. 34:27-35). Like Moses, Elijah also fasted forty days and nights, ascended Sinai

90

to meet with God and received a fresh commissioning for Israel. *"So he arose, and ate and drank; and he went in the strength of that food forty days and forty nights as far as Horeb, the mountain of God." (1 Kings 19:8)*

Given that what happened to Elijah on Mt. Sinai almost replicated what happened to Moses on that same mountain, this encounter in 1 Kings 19 was not just a moment of personal encouragement for Elijah, but a time of corporate shifting for the whole nation. What commenced on Carmel continued on Horeb. So from that place, what heavenly strategy was enacted? What divine commission was given?

The Lord told Elijah to anoint Hazael as king of Syria, Jehu as king of Israel and Elisha as prophet in his place. This verb *"anoint"* is *mashah* meaning to rub or smear particularly with oil, and that oil represents the Holy Spirit. Thus to be anointed is to be enabled by the Spirit to accomplish what one could not accomplish by his own strength, skill or ingenuity. It prepares a person to do the Lord's work, which is often impossible to do and requires the miraculous. *"Then Samuel took the horn of oil and anointed him in the midst of his brothers; and the Spirit of the Lord came upon David from that day forward." (1 Sam. 16:13) "The Spirit of the Lord is upon Me, because the Lord has anointed Me." (Isa. 61:1)*

These three men were anointed to finalize what Elijah began. However, the first two were kings, not prophets. In other words, God was going to further His work in Israel through political, military and governmental officials, not just through religious leaders.

The first was Hazael, who would become the king of Syria. While he was considered an enemy of Israel, in reality he was an instrument of the Lord. Through him God would continue to discipline the nation, and such discipline was a sign that God truly cared for His people. He would neither be aloof nor indifferent, but rather involved. This discipline would help maintain a level of humility, righteousness and justice that was fought for in the days of Elijah. *"In those days the Lord began to cut off parts of Israel; and Hazael conquered them in all the territory of Israel." (2 Kings 10:32)*

How, though, could a pagan king play such a role? How could a harsh ruler like Hazael be anointed by the Spirit and used by God? We need to see wider and higher purposes of God beyond our limited perspectives. We need to consider answers to prayer beyond our limited expectations. Transformation will come in ways we do not expect. For instance, in beholding the greatest act of God in history, which is the crucifixion and resurrection of His own Son, the apostles perceived the God-ordained roles of Herod, Pilate, the Gentiles and the Jews. All of these political leaders along with the people were woven into God's masterful and beautiful tapestry of redemption. *"For truly against Your holy Servant Jesus, whom You anointed, both Herod and Pontius Pilate, with the Gentiles and the people of Israel, were gathered together to do whatever Your hand and Your purpose determined before to be done." (Acts 4:27-28)*

The second was Jehu, who would become the king of Israel. Since the schism between Israel and Judah as detailed in 1 Kings 11-12, ten kings from Jeroboam to Joram ruled Israel from 930 to 841 B.C. Every one of those kings was said to do evil in the sight of the Lord (1 Kings 14:8-9; 15:26, 34; 16:19, 25, 30). Not one did what was right in God's sight, that is, not until Jehu, the eleventh king. Though Jehu was not perfect, he did do what was right in God's sight unlike all of his predecessors. Of him the Lord said, *"Because you have done well in doing what was right in My sight, and have done to the house of Ahab all that was in My heart, your sons shall sit on the throne of Israel to the fourth generation." (2 Kings 10:30)*

What did Jehu do that was right in God's sight? In what way did he obey the Lord? While Elijah was commissioned to anoint Jehu as king over Israel in 1 Kings 19:16, it was a man from the

Jehu means "Jehovah is he"

company of prophets who actually anointed Jehu at Elisha's request (2 Kings 9:1-10). Thus as the Spirit came upon Jehu, he fulfilled the Lord's will by slaying Jezebel (2 Kings 9:30-37), wiping out Ahab's family (10:1-17), and utterly destroying the ministers of Baal, the sacred stone of Baal, and the temple of Baal (10:18-30). To sum it up, the Scriptures declare, *"So Jehu destroyed Baal worship in Israel."* *(10:28 NIV)*

In other words, a great religious and spiritual shift began with the slaying of the prophets and prophetesses of Baal on Mt. Carmel under Elijah's leadership in 1 Kings 18, and that shift culminated with the final eradication of Baal worship from Israel under Jehu's leadership in 2 Kings 10. State-sanctioned Baal worship, with its demonic ideologies, corrupt officials and murderous practices, was removed from the land. This happened about twenty to thirty years after the confrontation on Mt. Carmel. Thus the effects of what happened in 1 Kings 18 were not just felt for days, but for decades following.

Prophets Brought Forth

"And Elisha the son of Shaphat of Abel Meholah you shall anoint as prophet in your place." 1 Kings 19:16

The third was Elisha, who would become the prophet in Elijah's stead. This was not just the filling of a vacant position, but the surging of a movement of the Spirit in the land. The anointing of Elisha would alter the spiritual landscape of Israel. The rivers of blessings would grow deeper, and the mountains of encounter would rise higher.

Elisha didn't just replace Elijah, but also surpassed him. God's desire is always for sons to outrun their fathers, and this should be every father's desire as well. Moses led Israel to the border of the promised land, but Joshua led them into it. David prepared for the construction of the temple, but Solomon actually built it. Jesus

93

worked the works of the Father, but His disciples were to do even greater works than His. *"The works that I do he will do also; and greater works than these he will do."* (*John 14:12*)

So Elisha didn't just ask for Elijah's anointing, but for a double portion of his spirit and power (2 Kings 2:9-15). He wasn't content just to walk in Elijah's footsteps, for he wanted to go even farther than his spiritual father. Elisha's request was granted, and of their prophecies and miracles recorded in Scripture, Elijah had about fourteen, yet Elisha about twenty-eight. Moreover, though Elisha carried the double portion, it was the nation of Israel that received the impact, influence and blessing of his expanded ministry.

Furthermore, this increase of the Spirit led to an increase of the number of prophets in the land as well. Large companies of prophets and prophetic apprentices developed and grew under Elisha's tutelage (2 Kings 2:15; 4:1, 38; 6:1; 9:1). For Israel, this meant a deeper and wider penetration of the word of the Lord in the nation. Simply put, more prophets meant more prophetic words, more miraculous works and a more powerful witness for the Lord in Israel and the surrounding nations.

A Nature like Ours

Elijah was a man with a nature like ours... James 5:17

As we look at Elijah's life and the extraordinary feats God accomplished through him, the thought of imitating him can be overwhelming, especially as we consider the breathtaking prophecies, miracles and demonstrations of power. Elijah's successes could easily intimidate any Christian earnestly pursuing such a lifestyle and course of ministry, yet let us remember that he was a human being just like us. He too struggled with fear, depression and feelings of loneliness and isolation (1 Kings 19:3-4, 10).

In other words, if God can use a weak, broken man like Elijah to turn a nation and prepare for divine visitation, then He can surely use you and me as well. Moreover, given the days in which we live, we must begin walking in the spirit and power of Elijah. We must become like John the Baptist in our generation. This is not just a fad or good idea, but God's mandate in this hour.

In the few days that I started typing my chapters for this book, except for my wife I told nobody about this writing project. Not one other person was aware of what I was writing. Given that, what I heard days later was remarkable.

During those same few days, a student with The Call School, which I direct, had an encounter with the Lord while in Kansas City. In it the Lord told her about the spirit of Elijah coming on this generation.

Also, during those same days, a member of our IHOP Strike Team, which is also a department I direct, had a dream from the Lord while on a prayer strike in Charlotte, North Carolina. In her dream two of her spiritual mothers were standing in front of her. She told them that she needed the mantle of Elijah, and so they proceeded to lay their hands upon her and pray. She remembered feeling that she really, really wanted that mantle.

Completely separate and independent of each other, days later both ladies told me what the Lord had revealed to them, and I was shocked and thrilled at the same time. God had confirmed to me in an unmistakable way the importance and urgency of this message in this historic hour. So let us not just read and study it, but also pray and live it! Now is the time.

CHAPTER 10

GOD SHED HIS GRACE ON THEE
(Lou Engle)

But where sin abounded, grace abounded much more. Romans 5:20

The Redemptive Judgments of God

Much has been said about Elijah the prophet, but his ministry would have failed apart from the redemptive judgments of God released through his word. No rain or dew would fall on Israel until the people return to the Lord and until the back of Baalism is broken. For three and a half years a drought and famine completely devastated the agrarian economic system of the apostate nation. It was the very judgment of God unleashed through the word of the prophet that would be used to turn the people back to Yahweh. This judgment would bring forth the destruction of all the prophets of Baal in the land and make war on Jezebel's witchcraft, bloodshed and sexual perversion. God was judging the gods and liberating the people from Baal's spiritual tyranny.

God has continued to confront our apostasy and the powers of darkness through seasons of tremendous judgment even in our own American history. Consider the Civil War, for the Missouri Compromise set in motion a series of events that would culminate in the bloodshed of six hundred thousand men in the war that would break the back of the heinous institution of slavery. When Abraham Lincoln was elected President, his main goal was not to end slavery but to preserve the Union. However, after four years of the war's scourge of death, he had experienced an ideological conversion. In his second inaugural address, he declared, *"Fondly do we hope - fervently do we pray - that this mighty scourge of war may speedily pass away. Yet, if God wills that it continue, until all the wealth piled by the bond-man's two hundred and fifty years of unrequited toil shall be sunk, and until every drop of blood drawn with the lash, shall be paid by another drawn with the sword, as was said three thousand years ago, so still it must be said 'the judgments of the Lord are true and righteous altogether.'"*

Do you see the insight of Lincoln? He was brought to an understanding of the doctrine of the shedding of innocent blood. *"Whoever sheds man's blood, by man his blood shall be shed; for in the image of God He made man." (Gen. 9:6)* He understood that the blood of the American soldiers was judicial retribution for the blood of the slaves and that God in His judgments was also breaking the economy of a nation that had built its prosperity on the bloody backs of its unpaid laborers.

James also gave voice to God's prophetic cry against economic injustice and slavery in the New Testament: *"Behold, the wages of the laborers who mowed your fields, which you kept back by fraud, are crying out against you and the cries of the harvesters have reached the ears of the Lord of hosts. You have lived on the earth in luxury and in self-indulgence. You have fattened your hearts in the day of slaughter." (James 5:4-5)*

It was this revelation that induced President Lincoln to release the Emancipation Proclamation. It was his proclamation to the Pharaohs of the south, *"Let my people go." (Exod. 5:1)* God calls it the day of vengeance and the year of redemption, for they go hand in hand. (Isa. 61:2) The God who marched forth in the Civil War in judgment against the shedding of blood was *"traveling in the greatness of His strength, mighty to save." (Isa. 63:1)* Justice and mercy were kissing each other. The same Son of Man who was crucified in the most outrageous display of love ever manifested is the same Son of God who prophesied the destruction of Jerusalem because of the Jewish leaders who killed the prophets that were sent to them. In seventy A.D. after the death of Jesus, the horrific destruction was carried out in fulfillment of His word. We believe that the judgments of the Lord, as in the days of Elijah, will break the back of abortion and bring forth a great returning to the Lord in America.

Remember the Unborn

What I am about to share with you is absolutely stunning. It is either a bad joke, or it is God. You must judge the prophecy. I pray you tremble at the sound as indeed the people of Joplin, MO, trembled when three tornados in one, a mile wide and six miles in length, roared through that town in Missouri on May 22, 2011.

When I read of the tornado and watched its devastation on television, I began to ponder the question, "Is this the redemptive judgment of God against the bloodshed of abortion?" I began to say to my friends, "Out of the Missouri Compromise once again God is marching forth and separating the nation with judgment and mercy to deal with the shedding of innocent blood of the unborn in America."

Soon after the tornado, Kirk Bennett, a leader at IHOP Kansas City, went down to assist the recovery operation in Joplin. Then in the providence of God he met a local pastor and leader of a house of prayer, Jim Marcum. This is Jim's story.

Eight weeks before the tornado, he was led by the Lord for the first time in his ministry to preach on the judgments of God, one of which was natural disasters, even tornados. Then six weeks before the tornado he had a dream.

> "I dreamed I was on a golf course, getting ready to tee off. I looked across from me, and there were President Obama and First Lady Michelle. They were also getting ready to tee off. I felt I should go and meet them, but instead I decided I would tee off first. When I hit the ball, it hooked left into some trees. I went to find my ball, and once I returned to the fairway I saw the President and First Lady were putting

on the green. I came walking toward them, and suddenly I began singing loudly the chorus to the song 'America, the Beautiful.' I was singing, 'America, America, God shed His grace on thee.' They were looking at me as I approached. Once I got to them, I became very emotional. I began to speak to the President, pleading with him to end abortion in America. I asked him to use the powers of his office to end the murders of innocent children in our nation. Neither he nor his wife seemed to know how to respond. I remember the vista in the background as I was speaking to them. It was of forests, mountains, and large bodies of water off in the distance, a panorama of the beauty that is in our nation. It seemed such a juxtaposition to see all this beauty as I was pleading with the President over the terrible ugliness that the blight of abortion has been on our nation."

Two weeks later Marcum's sixteen year old daughter had a dream. In it she walked into a building, and the atmosphere was very threatening and fearful. It was almost as if their lives were in danger. In this house, she was searching for a secret code. There she discovered a picture of Abraham Lincoln and illuminated on his face was the secret code, 5/29/11. Waking from the dream, a thought invaded her mind that she needed to go and read the Emancipation Proclamation. As she shared her dream with her parents they began to ponder the significance of this code. Was it a date? All that was left to do was to wait and ponder. Was a storyline being written?

On 5/22/11 the Joplin tornado struck, and on 5/29/11, the date of the secret code, President Obama came to Joplin. A citywide gathering was held, and the Marcums, because of the dream, attended. Actually, Jim was quite sick, but because of the revelation he felt he was to go. When the Marcum's arrived, there were no good seats. However, two pastors seated in the first row invited them to sit in their seats, the best seats because they were going to be on stage with the President.

When President Obama walked in through the door, immediately his eyes met Jim's. The President proceeded to the stage and delivered his message. He then stepped down off the stage and moved toward the front row to shake hands with the people seated there. Just as he was moving toward the Marcums, suddenly, the band kicked in with the song, "America, America, God shed His grace on thee," the very song he had heard in his dream.

He immediately turned to his wife and said, "It's the dream. I need to tell President Obama, 'You must end abortion.'" She replied, "If you don't, I will." As he shook the hand of President Obama, tears filled his eyes. He pleaded with him, "You must remember the unborn, you must remember the unborn!" The President seemed taken aback by the word and then walked on.

Shaking and Awakening

When I heard this story, I could hardly contain myself. If God is going to shed His grace on America, President Obama must end abortion. The interpretation began to be downloaded, I believe, from the Holy Spirit. President Lincoln was a man who presided over the nation under the redemptive judgments of God because of the shedding of the blood of the slaves. Now President Obama is the man presiding over a nation that is under the redemptive judgments of God for the shedding of the innocent blood of the unborn. Wouldn't it be like God to raise up a man from Illinois, President Lincoln, to release an Emancipation Proclamation to let the slaves go free so that a black man from Illinois, President Obama, could release an Emancipation Proclamation to let the unborn go free. We have criticized our President and pointed the finger at him, but I believe the survival of our nation may be determined by how we pray for him. What if God would use this man to bring about the reconciliation of black and white and the ending of abortion?

Please understand that I could never vote for anyone who

supports a governmental position empowering abortion. I believe that I would be an accomplice to murder. But in prayer for our governmental leaders we are called to shape history and bring peace to the nation. (1 Tim 2:1-6) I believe this year, 2012, is a year to pray for our President like never before to become a Lincoln-type President. It is a year to plead the blood of Jesus over our national sins and to call on God for mercy in the midst of the great shakings to come.

My whole heart has changed toward President Obama. I am praying for this man. I believe that as in Elijah's day, God is going to continue to break the economy in America. He wants to break the back of abortion in America. He loves this nation enough not to let it go on in its governmental rebellion and moral apostasy. We are entering an Elijah Revolution moment in which intercession, economic judgment and spiritual awakening will all converge. Someone recently said that 2012 and beyond will be a time of shaking and awakening, but if the church doesn't play her part, then only shaking.

Again my original interpretation of the dream was that Joplin was the beginning of a great separation being made in the nation over the issue of abortion. Amazingly, twenty-five of the streets that the tornado tore through in Joplin were named after states in America. Twenty-five states, one half of our fifty. God, I believe, chose Joplin as a sign to the nation. These are the days of Elijah.

Fast Forward Again

Burning with this dream and the intensity of a sense of the significance of 2012, we received another dream that had been given to one of the prophetic sons in Joplin, MO, in Marcum's house of prayer. In the dream, this young man was having a dream where he approached an antichrist-like being with major financial influence and control. It was a dream within a dream. Upon waking up, the scene changed, and he met President Obama and told him about the dream. The President, though, refused to hear the message and walked away.

Then handwriting on the wall appeared with the words, "LLOV Ezekiel 4:7-17." LLOV is the code for a large civilian and military airport in Israel. Ezekiel 4 describes a prophetic assignment given to the prophet Ezekiel. For three hundred ninety days, a day for every year of the iniquity of Israel, he was to eat nothing but bread made of wheat, barley, beans, lentils, millet and spelt. It was a prophetic declaration that God was going to judge Israel's apostasy with a famine and shortage of food resulting from the invasion of the Babylonians.

As I pondered this dream during Thanksgiving weekend in November, 2011, it suddenly occurred to me that I should subtract three hundred ninety years from that Thanksgiving holiday. It came to Thanksgiving weekend, 1621, the first Thanksgiving at Plymouth Rock. I was shocked. God are you calling me to three hundred ninety days of intercession to bear with You the iniquities for the three hundred ninety years of the sins of our nation, its shedding of native blood, slave blood and abortion blood?

I prayed, "God confirm this to me." I immediately opened my Bible, and my eyes fell on Ecclesiastes 11:1 (Please read the preface of this book). There it was again as in my Fast Forward assignment of 2000, *"Cast your bread upon the waters."* I wrote in my Bible, "390 Ezekiel bread fast."

Several days later I received an overwhelming sense that I had to go to Joplin immediately. I called my prophetic friend, Chris Berglund, who often dreams for me in key moments of my life, and asked him to go with me. That evening we prayed with the intercessors in Joplin and before going to bed in our separate hotel rooms, I asked God to give him a dream to confirm our three hundred ninety day prayer and fasting assignment. I had not told Chris about my Ecclesiastes 11:1 encounter and in fact had forgotten about it.

The next morning Chris shared the dream he had that previous night. In it, The Call community and Sam Cerny's team were gathered together in a time when the economy was totally broken in America. People were simply trying to survive. You could hardly trust anyone because of the financial collapse. At one point he walked up to Sam and hugged him, which I believe speaks of the joining of this prophetic prayer movement and the assignment of God that we are being given in 2012. He then turned to me and asked, "What is the Lord saying to you Lou?" And I responded, "He is saying to me, Ecclesiastes 11:1, cast your bread on the water."

When I heard the dream, I was astonished. No other word could have pierced me so intensely. A mantle of the Holy Spirit came over me, and I knew it was the word of the Lord. I immediately turned in my Bible to Ecclesiastes 11:1, and there was a note of mine written on the page, "Ezekiel bread fast 2012." I showed it to Chris, and we sat in stunned amazement. No one could have known what I had written in my Bible just days before.

2012 will be a massive transitional year. I believe that God was saying it is time to Fast Forward again and pray for 390 days for the President, for the ending of abortion, for another great awakening and then for something that I did not realize till just recently.

Three days before the Joplin tornado, President Obama released a statement calling Israel to divide Jerusalem and reinstate the pre-1967 boundaries of the city. Could the LLOV be bringing another prophetic dimension? Is God dealing with this nation on its bloodshed and its alliance with the nations of the earth against the covenant that God made with the people and land of Israel? Could Joplin be a great sign to America, to our President and to our government to tremble before Him and turn to Him? If Joplin, as it occurred to me, is only the beginning of signs of the judgments that are coming to this nation, what are we in store for in the coming season? A casual response to these prophetic warnings could be our undoing.

It is time to fast forward. In further confirmation to this prophetic assignment we are receiving, unbeknownst to me, Cindy Jacobs has called for a 384 day fast for America, ending on Inauguration Day 2013. And to bring the hammer down, she named it "Fast Forward." Unbelievable, unless of course it is God, and if it is, then we can believe for great mercy, a great awakening and maybe even a great reformation that will change the destiny of America.

Who knows? Maybe President Obama could be converted through the shakings of this year into an understanding of the doctrine of the shedding of innocent blood similar to Lincoln, so that in his second inaugural address, like Lincoln, he could deliver an Emancipation Proclamation for the unborn? Or maybe a reformation-minded, pro-life president could be elected who could bring a shift of times and seasons and laws giving America a dawning of a new day from abortion's tyranny?

Many may say this is an impossible dream. To this I say, only seven thousand out of millions had not bowed the knee to Baal. Yet even in that most wicked time of Israel's history, God brought forth her greatest prophet, Elijah, to bring a mighty revolution, and surely He can do it again today. He is the same yesterday, today and forever, and the promise of God is as bright today as when Malachi prophesied it two thousand four hundred years ago, *"Behold I will send you Elijah the prophet before the great and awesome day of the Lord comes. And He will turn the hearts of the fathers to their children and the hearts of the children to their fathers, lest I come and strike the land with a decree of utter destruction."* (Malachi 4:5-6)

APPENDIX
(Lou Engle)

Prayer Strategy

Join this fast forward for three hundred and ninety days into 2012 and beyond, and enter into a season of prayer and fasting during this transitional time for America and the nations.

1. *"Cast your bread upon the waters...For you do not know what evil will be on the earth." (Eccl. 11:1-2)* Let the Spirit give you a personal application for this verse. Some may want to do a grain diet as described in Ezek. 4:9. Others may want to avoid meats and sweets as depicted in Dan. 10:3. Follow the Lord however He leads you. Moreover, don't place yourself under a requirement that you cannot keep. If you falter, don't stay under condemnation. Grace! Press forward with the Lord's help.

2. Lessen the influence of movies, television, internet, video games and online social networking.

3. Follow online prayer and fasting communities such as thecall.com, ihop.org, generals.org or other similar ministries.

4. Mobilize churches, youth groups, colleges or Christian clubs to fast and pray.

Prayer Focuses

1. Pray for a personal cleansing from sexual impurity, materialism, pride and rebellion to break the seductive, Jezebel-like influence permeating the world around us.

2. Pray for this Elijah generation to receive a double portion of the gifts, fruit and wisdom of the Holy Spirit.

3. Pray for President Obama and leaders of nations across the

earth to become Lincoln-type leaders who would release Emancipation Proclamations to let the unborn go free and to stand with the Jewish people and God's commitment to them and their land.

4. Pray for another great awakening, where millions of souls would come to Christ.

5. Pray for specific young people, those "dead kids" you know, that they would be raised from the dead, so to speak, and be delivered from their bondages.

6. Pray for a turning of the hearts of the fathers to the children and the children to their fathers, for an Elijah revolution.

7. Pray against divorce and for renewal of marriages in America and the nations.

8. Find your Elisha and pour your life into him or her.

Fasting Suggestions

1. *Fast and pray in order to humble yourself and purify your worship.* In fasting we are not trying to get something from God, but rather seeking to realign our hearts' affections with His. We do holy violence to the "pleasures which wage war against the soul," opening the way for a greater submission to the Holy Spirit. In fasting we can more readily say, "We love you, Lord, more than anything in the world." Lust of any kind is perverted worship, but fasting enables us to cleanse the sanctuary of our hearts from every other rival.

2. *Take time to pray and read the Word.* This may seem obvious, but busyness and distractions can keep you from devotions. Reading books with testimonies of victories gained through fasting will encourage you.

3. *Have a clear target for prayer focus.* Without a vision (a clear, prophetic prayer goal) the people perish. During a fast I have four or five prayer goals that are

clearly articulated. When I'm not deeply motivated by a clear goal, I usually fast until break-fast! Write down your vision, so you can run with it.

4. *Do the fast with someone else.*
   Two are better than one! We encourage young people to talk this through with their parents before starting the fast. Parents and kids should consider fasting together.

5. *If you fail, don't give in to condemnation.*
   The "to fast or not to fast" dilemma can be a major tool of the enemy. Even though you may fail several times, God always extends grace. Once, I gave up on my fast and snuck some yogurt and chips. The next day an intercessor came to me and said, "I saw you in a dream and you were supposed to be fasting, but you were eating yogurt and chips." That was a pretty good motivation to start again!

6. *Parents, consider sexual abstinence for the sake of prayer. (1 Cor. 7:5)*

7. *Make your commitment and determine the length.*
   … A total fast is without water. Don't go beyond three days.
   … A water-only fast is very difficult, but very effective. Depending on your weight and metabolism, you can go forty days on water alone.
   … A fruit or vegetable juice fast allows you to enter into fasting but still gives enough energy to function. Most people can do a 40-day juice fast. Out of consideration for their health and metabolism, I would encourage teenagers to use juice and protein drinks to sustain them.

8. *Prepare physically.*
   Two days before you fast, limit your intake of food to fruit and vegetables. Fruit is a natural cleanser and easy to digest. Stop drinking coffee *before* the fast. Prepare yourself for

mental discomforts such as impatience, crankiness and anxiety. Expect physical discomforts. You may experience dizziness, headaches and different kinds of pains. The headaches are not a sign to stop fasting. Your body is working to cleanse itself of impurities.

9. *Prepare for opposition.*
On the day of your fast you can bet donuts will be at the office or in class. Your spouse (or mom) will suddenly be inspired to cook your favorite meals. Press through. Many times you may feel more tension build up at home. My fasts are just as difficult for my wife as they are for me. Satan tempted Jesus on the fast, and we must expect the same. Discouragement may come in like a flood, but recognize the source and take your stand on the victory of Christ.

10. *Fast in secret.*
Don't boast about your fast, but let people know you won't be eating, if you need to.

11. *Break the fast over several days with fruit juice or light soups.*
On a light juice fast or a water fast your digestive system shuts down. This can be dangerous if you eat too much too soon. Break the fast with several days of diluted, non-acidic juice, then regular juice, followed by fruit and vegetables. On one of my early water fasts, I broke it too quickly and almost needed hospitalization. Be careful!

12. *Feel free to rest a lot and to continue to exercise.*

13. *Seek medical advice if you are older or have any type of health challenges.*

14. *Expect to hear God's voice in the Word, dreams, visions, and revelations.*
Daniel prepared himself to receive revelation through fasting (Dan. 10:1-2). There is a fasting reward (Matt. 6:18). Some

time ago, a Malaysian brother shared how during a forty day fast he was "caught up into the heavens." After the fast, he took a team into the interior of Borneo and saw a dead woman raised, and revival broke out in the village.

15. *Breakthroughs often come after a fast, not during it.*
Do not listen to the lie that nothing is happening. It is my conviction that every fast done in faith will be rewarded.

May thousands of young men and women fast, as God leads them, finding a greater intimacy with God the Father. May they be used in the greatest revival we have ever seen. Let two generations arise and fulfill this divine mandate. We have taught our children how to feast and play. Now it is time to teach them to fast and pray! The forty-day fast is not just an historic eccentricity in the Bible. It is a model, and I believe it is a call for the last days generation, standing at the crossroads of time. As we cross over this next threshold, let's *Fast Forward!*